# AS YOU LIKE IT

*William Shakespeare*

# A Prologue from the Bard

Brave scholars, blessed with time and energy,
    At school, fair Harvard, set about to glean,
From dusty tomes and modern poetry,
    All truths and knowledge formerly unseen.
From forth the hungry minds of these good folk
    Study guides, star-floss'd, soon came to life;
Whose deep and deft analysis awoke
    The latent "A"s of those in lit'rary strife.
Aim far past passing—insight from our trove
    Will free your comprehension from its cage.
Our SparkNotes' worth, online we also prove;
    Behold this book! Same brains, but paper page.
If patient or "whatever," please attend,
    What you have missed, our toil shall strive to mend.

# Contents

# Context

T HE MOST INFLUENTIAL WRITER in all of English literature, William Shakespeare was born in 1564 to a
successful middle-class glover in Stratford-upon-Avon,
England. Shakespeare attended grammar school, but his
formal education proceeded no further. In 1582 he married an older woman, Anne Hathaway, and had three children with
her. Around 1590, he left his family behind and traveled to London
to work as an actor and playwright. Public and critical acclaim
quickly followed, and Shakespeare eventually became the most
popular playwright in England and part-owner of the Globe Theater. His career bridged the reigns of Elizabeth I (ruled 1558–1603)
and James I (ruled 1603–1625), and he was a favorite of both mon-
archs. Indeed, James granted Shakespeare's company the greatest
possible compliment by bestowing upon its members the title of
King's Men. Wealthy and renowned, Shakespeare retired to Strat-
ford and died in 1616 at the age of fifty-two. At the time of Shakespeare's death, literary luminaries such as Ben Jonson hailed his
works as timeless.

Shakespeare's works were collected and printed in various
editions in the century following his death, and by the early eigh-
teenth century, his reputation as the greatest poet ever to write in
English was well established. The unprecedented admiration gar-
nered by his works led to a fierce curiosity about Shakespeare's life,
but the dearth of biographical information has left many details of
Shakespeare's personal history shrouded in mystery. Some people
have concluded from this fact and from Shakespeare's modest education that Shakespeare's plays were actually written by someone
else—Francis Bacon and the Earl of Oxford are the two most popular candidates—but the support for this claim is overwhelmingly
circumstantial, and the theory is not taken seriously by many scholars.

In the absence of credible evidence to the contrary, Shakespeare
must be viewed as the author of the thirty-seven plays and 154 son-
nets that bear his name. The legacy of this body of work is immense.
A number of Shakespeare's plays seem to have transcended even the
category of brilliance, becoming so influential as to affect pro-
foundly the course of Western literature and culture ever after.

*As You Like It* was most likely written around 1598–1600, during the last years of Elizabeth's reign. The play belongs to the literary tradition known as *pastoral:* which has its roots in the literature of ancient Greece, came into its own in Roman antiquity with Virgil's *Eclogues,* and continued as a vital literary mode through Shakespeare's time and long after. Typically, a pastoral story involves exiles from urban or court life who flee to the refuge of the countryside, where they often disguise themselves as shepherds in order to converse with other shepherds on a range of established topics, from the relative merits of life at court versus life in the country to the relationship between nature and art. The most fundamental concern of the pastoral mode is comparing the worth of the natural world, represented by relatively untouched countryside, to the world built by humans, which contains the joys of art and the city as well as the injustices of rigid social hierarchies. Pastoral literature, then, has great potential to serve as a forum for social criticism and can even inspire social reform.

In general, Shakespeare's *As You Like It* develops many of the traditional features and concerns of the pastoral genre. This comedy examines the cruelties and corruption of court life and gleefully pokes holes in one of humankind's greatest artifices: the conventions of romantic love. The play's investment in pastoral traditions leads to an indulgence in rather simple rivalries: court versus country, realism versus romance, reason versus mindlessness, nature versus fortune, young versus old, and those who are born into nobility versus those who acquire their social standing. But rather than settle these scores by coming down on one side or the other, *As You Like It* offers up a world of myriad choices and endless possibilities. In the world of this play, no one thing need cancel out another. In this way, the play manages to offer both social critique and social affirmation. It is a play that at all times stresses the complexity of things, the simultaneous pleasures and pains of being human.

# PLOT OVERVIEW

S IR ROWLAND DE BOIS HAS RECENTLY DIED, and, according to the custom of primogeniture, the vast majority of his estate has passed into the possession of his eldest son, Oliver. Although Sir Rowland has instructed Oliver to take good care of his brother, Orlando, Oliver refuses to do so. Out of pure spite, he denies Orlando the education, training, and property befitting a gentleman. Charles, a wrestler from the court of Duke Frederick, arrives to warn Oliver of a rumor that Orlando will challenge Charles to a fight on the following day. Fearing censure if he should beat a nobleman, Charles begs Oliver to intervene, but Oliver convinces the wrestler that Orlando is a dishonorable sportsman who will take whatever dastardly means necessary to win. Charles vows to pummel Orlando, which delights Oliver.

Duke Senior has been usurped of his throne by his brother, Duke Frederick, and has fled to the Forest of Ardenne, where he lives like Robin Hood with a band of loyal followers. Duke Frederick allows Senior's daughter, Rosalind, to remain at court because of her inseparable friendship with his own daughter, Celia. The day arrives when Orlando is scheduled to fight Charles, and the women witness Orlando's defeat of the court wrestler. Orlando and Rosalind instantly fall in love with one another, though Rosalind keeps this fact a secret from everyone but Celia. Orlando returns home from the wrestling match, only to have his faithful servant Adam warn him about Oliver's plot against Orlando's life. Orlando decides to leave for the safety of Ardenne. Without warning, Duke Frederick has a change of heart regarding Rosalind and banishes her from court. She, too, decides to flee to the Forest of Ardenne and leaves with Celia, who cannot bear to be without Rosalind, and Touchstone, the court jester. To ensure the safety of their journey, Rosalind assumes the dress of a young man and takes the name Ganymede, while Celia dresses as a common shepherdess and calls herself Aliena.

Duke Frederick is furious at his daughter's disappearance. When he learns that the flight of his daughter and niece coincides with the disappearance of Orlando, the duke orders Oliver to lead the manhunt, threatening to confiscate Oliver's lands and property should he fail. Frederick also decides it is time to destroy his brother once and for all and begins to raise an army.

Duke Senior lives in the Forest of Ardenne with a band of lords who have gone into voluntary exile. He praises the simple life among the trees, happy to be absent from the machinations of court life. Orlando, exhausted by travel and desperate to find food for his starving companion, Adam, barges in on the duke's camp and rudely demands that they not eat until he is given food. Duke Senior calms Orlando and, when he learns that the young man is the son of his dear former friend, accepts him into his company. Meanwhile, Rosalind and Celia, disguised as Ganymede and Aliena, arrive in the forest and meet a lovesick young shepherd named Silvius who pines away for the disdainful Phoebe. The two women purchase a modest cottage, and soon enough Rosalind runs into the equally lovesick Orlando. Taking her to be a young man, Orlando confides in Rosalind that his affections are overpowering him. Rosalind, as Ganymede, claims to be an expert in exorcising such emotions and promises to cure Orlando of lovesickness if he agrees to pretend that Ganymede is Rosalind and promises to come woo her every day. Orlando agrees, and the love lessons begin.

Meanwhile, Phoebe becomes increasingly cruel in her rejection of Silvius. When Rosalind intervenes, disguised as Ganymede, Phoebe falls hopelessly in love with Ganymede. One day, Orlando fails to show up for his tutorial with Ganymede. Rosalind, reacting to her infatuation with Orlando, is distraught until Oliver appears. Oliver describes how Orlando stumbled upon him in the forest and saved him from being devoured by a hungry lioness. Oliver and Celia, still disguised as the shepherdess Aliena, fall instantly in love and agree to marry. As time passes, Phoebe becomes increasingly insistent in her pursuit of Ganymede, and Orlando grows tired of pretending that a boy is his dear Rosalind. Rosalind decides to end the charade. She promises that Ganymede will wed Phoebe, if Ganymede will ever marry a woman, and she makes everyone pledge to meet the next day at the wedding. They all agree.

The day of the wedding arrives, and Rosalind gathers the various couples: Phoebe and Silvius; Celia and Oliver; Touchstone and Audrey, a goatherd he intends to marry; and Orlando. The group congregates before Duke Senior and his men. Rosalind, still disguised as Ganymede, reminds the lovers of their various vows, then secures a promise from Phoebe that if for some reason she refuses to marry Ganymede she will marry Silvius, and a promise from the duke that he would allow his daughter to marry Orlando if she were available. Rosalind leaves with the disguised Celia, and the two soon return as themselves, accompanied by Hymen, the god of marriage. Hymen officiates at the ceremony and marries Rosalind and Orlando, Celia and Oliver, Phoebe and Silvius, and Audrey and Touchstone. The festive wedding celebration is interrupted by even more festive news: while marching with his army to attack Duke Senior, Duke Frederick came upon a holy man who convinced him to put aside his worldly concerns and assume a monastic life. Frederick changes his ways and returns the throne to Duke Senior. The guests continue dancing, happy in the knowledge that they will soon return to the royal court.

# CHARACTER LIST

*Rosalind*    The daughter of Duke Senior. Rosalind, considered one of Shakespeare's most delightful heroines, is independent minded, strong-willed, good-hearted, and terribly clever. Rather than slink off into defeated exile, Rosalind resourcefully uses her trip to the Forest of Ardenne as an opportunity to take control of her own destiny. When she disguises herself as Ganymede—a handsome young man—and offers herself as a tutor in the ways of love to her beloved Orlando, Rosalind's talents and charms are on full display. Only Rosalind, for instance, is both aware of the foolishness of romantic love *and* delighted to be in love. She teaches those around her to think, feel, and love better than they have previously, and she ensures that the courtiers returning from Ardenne are far gentler than those who fled to it.

*Orlando*    The youngest son of Sir Rowland de Bois and younger brother of Oliver. Orlando is an attractive young man who, under his brother's neglectful care, has languished without a gentleman's education or training. Regardless, he considers himself to have great potential, and his victorious battle with Charles proves him right. Orlando cares for the aging Adam in the Forest of Ardenne and later risks his life to save Oliver from a hungry lioness, proving himself a proper gentleman. He is a fitting hero for the play and, though he proves no match for her wit or poetry, the most obvious romantic match for Rosalind.

*Duke Senior*  The father of Rosalind and the rightful ruler of the dukedom in which the play is set. Having been banished by his usurping brother, Frederick, Duke Senior now lives in exile in the Forest of Ardenne with a number of loyal men, including Lord Amiens and Jaques. We have the sense that Senior did not put up much of a fight to keep his dukedom, for he seems to make the most of whatever life gives him. Content in the forest, where he claims to learn as much from stones and brooks as he would in a church or library, Duke Senior proves himself to be a kind and fair-minded ruler.

*Jaques*  A faithful lord who accompanies Duke Senior into exile in the Forest of Ardenne. Jaques is an example of a stock figure in Elizabethan comedy, the man possessed of a hopelessly melancholy disposition. Much like a referee in a football game, he stands on the sidelines, watching and judging the actions of the other characters without ever fully participating. Given his inability to participate in life, it is fitting that Jaques alone refuses to follow Duke Senior and the other courtiers back to court, and instead resolves to assume a solitary and contemplative life in a monastery.

*Celia*  The daughter of Duke Frederick and Rosalind's dearest friend. Celia's devotion to Rosalind is unmatched, as evidenced by her decision to follow her cousin into exile. To make the trip, Celia assumes the disguise of a simple shepherdess and calls herself Aliena. As elucidated by her extreme love of Rosalind and her immediate devotion to Oliver, whom she marries at the end of the play, Celia possesses a loving heart, but is prone to deep, almost excessive emotions.

*Duke Frederick*  The brother of Duke Senior and usurper of his throne. Duke Frederick's cruel nature and volatile temper are displayed when he banishes his niece, Rosalind, from court without reason. That Celia, his own daughter, cannot mitigate his unfounded anger demonstrates the intensity of the duke's hatefulness. Frederick mounts an army against his exiled brother but aborts his vengeful mission after he meets an old religious man on the road to the Forest of Ardenne. He immediately changes his ways, dedicating himself to a monastic life and returning the crown to his brother, thus testifying to the ease and elegance with which humans can sometimes change for the better.

*Touchstone*  A clown in Duke Frederick's court who accompanies Rosalind and Celia in their flight to Ardenne. Although Touchstone's job, as fool, is to criticize the behavior and point out the folly of those around him, Touchstone fails to do so with even a fraction of Rosalind's grace. Next to his mistress, the clown seems hopelessly vulgar and narrow-minded. Almost every line he speaks echoes with bawdy innuendo.

*Oliver*  The oldest son of Sir Rowland de Bois and sole inheritor of the de Bois estate. Oliver is a loveless young man who begrudges his brother, Orlando, a gentleman's education. He admits to hating Orlando without cause or reason and goes to great lengths to ensure his brother's downfall. When Duke Frederick employs Oliver to find his missing brother, Oliver finds himself living in despair in the Forest of Ardenne, where Orlando saves his life. This display of undeserved generosity prompts Oliver to change himself into a better, more loving person. His transformation is evidenced by his love for the disguised Celia, whom he takes to be a simple shepherdess.

*Silvius*  A young, suffering shepherd, who is desperately in love with the disdainful Phoebe. Conforming to the model of Petrarchan love, Silvius prostrates himself before a woman who refuses to return his affections. In the end, however, he wins the object of his desire.

*Phoebe*  A young shepherdess, who disdains the affections of Silvius. She falls in love with Ganymede, who is really Rosalind in disguise, but Rosalind tricks Phoebe into marrying Silvius.

*Lord Amiens*  A faithful lord who accompanies Duke Senior into exile in the Forest of Ardenne. Lord Amiens is rather jolly and loves to sing.

*Charles*    A professional wrestler in Duke Frederick's court. Charles demonstrates both his caring nature and his political savvy when he asks Oliver to intercede in his upcoming fight with Orlando: he does not want to injure the young man and thereby lose favor among the nobles who support him. Charles's concern for Orlando proves unwarranted when Orlando beats him senseless.

*Adam*    The elderly former servant of Sir Rowland de Bois. Having witnessed Orlando's hardships, Adam offers not only to accompany his young master into exile but to fund their journey with the whole of his modest life's savings. He is a model of loyalty and devoted service.

*Sir Rowland de Bois*    The father of Oliver and Orlando, friend of Duke Senior, and enemy of Duke Frederick. Upon Sir Rowland's death, the vast majority of his estate was handed over to Oliver according to the custom of primogeniture.

*Corin*    A shepherd. Corin attempts to counsel his friend Silvius in the ways of love, but Silvius refuses to listen.

*Audrey*    A simpleminded goatherd who agrees to marry Touchstone.

*William*    A young country boy who is in love with Audrey.

# ANALYSIS OF MAJOR CHARACTERS

## ROSALIND

Rosalind dominates *As You Like It*. So fully realized is she in the complexity of her emotions, the subtlety of her thought, and the fullness of her character that no one else in the play matches up to her. Orlando is handsome, strong, and an affectionate, if unskilled, poet, yet still we feel that Rosalind settles for someone slightly less magnificent when she chooses him as her mate. Similarly, the observations of Touchstone and Jaques, who might shine more brightly in another play, seem rather dull whenever Rosalind takes the stage.

The endless appeal of watching Rosalind has much to do with her success as a knowledgeable and charming critic of herself and others. But unlike Jaques, who refuses to participate wholly in life but has much to say about the foolishness of those who surround him, Rosalind gives herself over fully to circumstance. She chastises Silvius for his irrational devotion to Phoebe, and she challenges Orlando's thoughtless equation of Rosalind with a Platonic ideal, but still she comes undone by her lover's inconsequential tardiness and faints at the sight of his blood. That Rosalind can play both sides of any field makes her identifiable to nearly everyone, and so, irresistible.

Rosalind is a particular favorite among feminist critics, who admire her ability to subvert the limitations that society imposes on her as a woman. With boldness and imagination, she disguises herself as a young man for the majority of the play in order to woo the man she loves and instruct him in how to be a more accomplished, attentive lover—a tutorship that would not be welcome from a woman. There is endless comic appeal in Rosalind's lampooning of the conventions of both male and female behavior, but an Elizabethan audience might have felt a certain amount of anxiety regarding her behavior. After all, the structure of a male-dominated society depends upon both men and women acting in their assigned roles. Thus, in the end, Rosalind dispenses with the charade of her own character. Her emergence as an actor in the Epilogue assures that theatergoers, like the Ardenne foresters, are about to exit a some-what enchanted realm and return to the familiar world they left behind. But because they leave having learned the same lessons from Rosalind, they do so with the same potential to make that world a less punishing place.

## ORLANDO

According to his brother, Oliver, Orlando is of noble character, unschooled yet somehow learned, full of noble purposes, and loved by people of all ranks as if he had enchanted them (I.i.141–144). Although this description comes from the one character who hates Orlando and wishes him harm, it is an apt and generous picture of the hero of *As You Like It*. Orlando has a brave and generous spirit, though he does not possess Rosalind's wit and insight. As his love tutorial shows, he relies on commonplace clichés in matters of love, declaring that without the fair Rosalind, he would die. He does have a decent wit, however, as he demonstrates when he argues with Jaques, suggesting that Jaques should seek out a fool who wanders about the forest: "He is drowned in the brook. Look but in, and you shall see him," meaning that Jaques will see a fool in his own reflection (III.ii.262–263). But next to Rosalind, Orlando's imagination burns a bit less bright. This upstaging is no fault of Orlando's, given the fullness of Rosalind's character; Shakespeare clearly intends his audience to delight in the match. Time and again, Orlando performs tasks that reveal his nobility and demonstrate why he is so well-loved: he travels with the ancient Adam and makes a fool out of himself to secure the old man food; he risks his life to save the brother who has plotted against him; he cannot help but violate the many trees of Ardenne with testaments of his love for Rosalind. In the beginning of the play, he laments that his brother has denied him the schooling deserved by a gentleman, but by the end, he has proven himself a gentleman without the formality of that education.

## JAQUES

Jaques delights in being sad—a disparate role in a play that so delights in happiness. Jaques believes that his melancholy makes him the perfect candidate to be Duke Senior's fool. Such a position, he claims, will "Give me leave / To speak my mind," and the criticism that flows forth will "Cleanse the foul body of th'infected world" (II.vii.58–60). Duke Senior is rightly cautious about install-ing Jaques as the fool, fearing that Jaques would do little more than excoriate the sins that Jaques himself has committed. Indeed, Jaques lacks the keenness of insight of Shakespeare's most accomplished jesters: he is not as penetrating as *Twelfth Night*'s Feste or *King Lear*'s fool. In fact, he is more like an aspiring fool than a profes-sional one. When Jaques philosophizes on the seven stages of human life, for instance, his musings strike us as banal. His "All the world's a stage" speech is famous today, but the play itself casts doubt on the ideas expressed in this speech (II.vii.138). No sooner does Jaques insist that man spends the final stages of his life in "mere oblivion, / Sans teeth, sans eyes, sans taste, sans everything" than Orlando's aged servant, Adam, enters, bearing with him his loyalty, his incomparable service, and his undiminished integrity (II.vii.164–165).

Jaques's own faculties as a critic of the goings-on around him are considerably diminished in comparison to Rosalind, who under-stands so much more and conveys her understanding with superior grace and charm. Rosalind criticizes in order to transform the world—to make Orlando a more reasonable husband and Phoebe a less disdainful lover—whereas Jaques is content to stew in his own melancholy. It is appropriate that Jaques decides not to return to court. While the other characters merrily revel, Jaques determines that he will follow the reformed Duke Frederick into the monastery, where he believes the converts have much to teach him. Jaques's refusal to resume life in the dukedom not only confirms our impres-sion of his character, but also resonates with larger issues in the play. Here, the play makes good on the promise of its title: everyone gets just what he or she wants. It also betrays a small but inevitable crack in the community that dances through the forest. In a world as com-plex and full of so many competing forces as the one portrayed in *As You Like It,* the absolute best one can hope for is consensus, but never complete unanimity.

# THEMES, MOTIFS & SYMBOLS

## THEMES

*Themes are the fundamental and often universal ideas explored in a literary work.*

### THE DELIGHTS OF LOVE

*As You Like It* spoofs many of the conventions of poetry and literature dealing with love, such as the idea that love is a disease that brings suffering and torment to the lover, or the assumption that the male lover is the slave or servant of his mistress. These ideas are central features of the courtly love tradition, which greatly influenced European literature for hundreds of years before Shakespeare's time. In *As You Like It*, characters lament the suffering caused by their love, but these laments are all unconvincing and ridiculous. While Orlando's metrically incompetent poems conform to the notion that he should "live and die [Rosalind's] slave," these sentiments are roundly ridiculed (III.ii.142). Even Silvius, the untutored shepherd, assumes the role of the tortured lover, asking his beloved Phoebe to notice "the wounds invisible / That love's keen arrows make" (III.v.31–32). But Silvius's request for Phoebe's attention implies that the enslaved lover can loosen the chains of love and that all romantic wounds can be healed—otherwise, his request for notice would be pointless. In general, *As You Like It* breaks with the courtly love tradition by portraying love as a force for happiness and fulfillment and ridicules those who revel in their own suffering.

Celia speaks to the curative powers of love in her introductory scene with Rosalind, in which she implores her cousin to allow "the full weight" of her love to push aside Rosalind's unhappy thoughts (I.ii.6). As soon as Rosalind takes to Ardenne, she displays her own copious knowledge of the ways of love. Disguised as Ganymede, she tutors Orlando in how to be a more attentive and caring lover, counsels Silvius against prostrating himself for the sake of the all-too-human Phoebe, and scolds Phoebe for her arrogance in playing the shepherd's disdainful love object. When Rosalind famously insists that "[m]en have died from time to time, and worms have eaten them, but not for love," she argues against the notion that love concerns the perfect, mythic, or unattainable (IV.i.91–92). Unlike Jaques and Touchstone, both of whom have keen eyes and biting tongues trained on the follies of romance, Rosalind does not mean to disparage love. On the contrary, she seeks to teach a version of love that not only can survive in the real world, but can bring delight as well. By the end of the play, having successfully orchestrated four marriages and ensured the happy and peaceful return of a more just government, Rosalind proves that love is a source of incomparable delight.

### The Malleability of the Human Experience

In Act II, scene vii, Jaques philosophizes on the stages of human life: man passes from infancy into boyhood; becomes a lover, a soldier, and a wise civic leader; and then, year by year, becomes a bit more foolish until he is returned to his "second childishness and mere oblivion" (II.vii.164). Jaques's speech remains an eloquent commentary on how quickly and thoroughly human beings can change, and, indeed, *do* change in *As You Like It*. Whether physically, emotionally, or spiritually, those who enter the Forest of Ardenne are often remarkably different when they leave. The most dramatic and unmistakable change, of course, occurs when Rosalind assumes the disguise of Ganymede. As a young man, Rosalind demonstrates how vulnerable to change men and women truly are. Orlando, of course, is putty in her hands; more impressive, however, is her ability to manipulate Phoebe's affections, which move from Ganymede to the once despised Silvius with amazing speed.

In *As You Like It*, Shakespeare dispenses with the time-consuming and often hard-won processes involved in change. The characters do not struggle to become more pliant—their changes are instantaneous. Oliver, for instance, learns to love both his brother Orlando and a disguised Celia within moments of setting foot in the forest. Furthermore, the vengeful and ambitious Duke Frederick abandons all thoughts of fratricide after a single conversation with a religious old man. Certainly, these transformations have much to do with the restorative, almost magical effects of life in the forest, but the consequences of the changes also matter in the real world: the government that rules the French duchy, for example, will be more just under the rightful ruler Duke Senior, while the class structures inherent in court life promise to be somewhat less rigid after the courtiers sojourn in the forest. These social reforms are a clear improvement and result from the more private reforms of the play's characters. *As You Like It* not only insists that people can and do change, but also celebrates their ability to change for the better.

### CITY LIFE VERSUS COUNTRY LIFE

Pastoral literature thrives on the contrast between life in the city and life in the country. Often, it suggests that the oppressions of the city can be remedied by a trip into the country's therapeutic woods and fields, and that a person's sense of balance and rightness can be restored by conversations with uncorrupted shepherds and shepherdesses. This type of restoration, in turn, enables one to return to the city a better person, capable of making the most of urban life. Although Shakespeare tests the bounds of these conventions—his shepherdess Audrey, for instance, is neither articulate nor pure—he begins *As You Like It* by establishing the city/country dichotomy on which the pastoral mood depends. In Act I, scene i, Orlando rails against the injustices of life with Oliver and complains that he "know[s] no wise remedy how to avoid it" (I.i.20–21). Later in that scene, as Charles relates the whereabouts of Duke Senior and his followers, the remedy is clear: "in the forest of Ardenne . . . many young gentlemen . . . fleet the time carelessly, as they did in the golden world" (I.i.99–103). Indeed, many are healed in the forest—the lovesick are coupled with their lovers and the usurped duke returns to his throne—but Shakespeare reminds us that life in Ardenne is a temporary affair. As the characters prepare to return to life at court, the play does not laud country over city or vice versa, but instead suggests a delicate and necessary balance between the two. The simplicity of the forest provides shelter from the strains of the court, but it also creates the need for urban style and sophistication: one would not do, or even matter, without the other.

## MOTIFS

> *Motifs are recurring structures, contrasts, or literary devices that can help to develop and inform the text's major themes.*

### ARTIFICE

As Orlando runs through the forest decorating every tree with love poems for Rosalind, and as Silvius pines for Phoebe and compares her cruel eyes to a murderer, we cannot help but notice the impor-

MOTIFS

tance of artifice to life in Ardenne. Phoebe decries such artificiality when she laments that her eyes lack the power to do the devoted shepherd any real harm, and Rosalind similarly puts a stop to Orlando's romantic fussing when she reminds him that "[m]en have died from time to time, and worms have eaten them, but not for love" (IV.i.91–92). Although Rosalind is susceptible to the contrivances of romantic love, as when her composure crumbles when Orlando is only minutes late for their appointment, she does her best to move herself and the others toward a more realistic understanding of love. Knowing that the excitement of the first days of courtship will flag, she warns Orlando that "[m]aids are May when they are maids, but the sky changes when they are wives" (IV.i.125–127). Here, Rosalind cautions against any love that sustains itself on artifice alone. She advocates a love that, while delightful, can survive in the real world. During the Epilogue, Rosalind returns the audience to reality by stripping away not only the artifice of Ardenne, but of her character as well. As the Elizabethan actor stands on the stage and reflects on this temporary foray into the unreal, the audience's experience comes to mirror the experience of the characters. The theater becomes Ardenne, the artful means of edifying us for our journey into the world in which we live.

### HOMOEROTICISM

Like many of Shakespeare's plays and poems, *As You Like It* explores different kinds of love between members of the same sex. Celia and Rosalind, for instance, are extremely close friends—almost sisters—and the profound intimacy of their relationship seems at times more intense than that of ordinary friends. Indeed, Celia's words in Act I, scenes ii and iii echo the protestations of lovers. But to assume that Celia or Rosalind possesses a sexual identity as clearly defined as our modern understandings of *heterosexual* or *homosexual* would be to work against the play's celebration of a range of intimacies and sexual possibilities.

The other kind of homoeroticism within the play arises from Rosalind's cross-dressing. Everybody, male and female, seems to love Ganymede, the beautiful boy who looks like a woman because he is really Rosalind in disguise. The name Rosalind chooses for her alter ego, Ganymede, traditionally belonged to a beautiful boy who became one of Jove's lovers, and the name carries strong homosexual connotations. Even though Orlando is supposed to be in love with Rosalind, he seems to enjoy the idea of acting out his romance with the beautiful, young boy Ganymede—almost as if a boy who looks like the woman he loves is even more appealing than the woman herself. Phoebe, too, is more attracted to the feminine Ganymede than to the real male, Silvius.

In drawing on the motif of homoeroticism, *As You Like It* is influenced by the pastoral tradition, which typically contains elements of same-sex love. In the Forest of Ardenne, as in pastoral literature, homoerotic relationships are not necessarily antithetical to heterosexual couplings, as modern readers tend to assume. Instead, homosexual and heterosexual love exist on a continuum across which, as the title of the play suggests, one can move as one likes.

### Exile

*As You Like It* abounds in banishment. Some characters have been forcibly removed or threatened from their homes, such as Duke Senior, Rosalind, and Orlando. Some have voluntarily abandoned their positions out of a sense of rightness, such as Senior's loyal band of lords, Celia, and the noble servant Adam. It is, then, rather remarkable that the play ends with four marriages—a ceremony that unites individuals into couples and ushers these couples into the community. The community that sings and dances its way through Ardenne at the close of Act V, scene iv, is the same community that will return to the dukedom in order to rule and be ruled. This event, where the poor dance in the company of royalty, suggests a utopian world in which wrongs can be righted and hurts healed. The sense of restoration with which the play ends depends upon the formation of a community of exiles in politics and love coming together to soothe their various wounds.

## Symbols

*Symbols are objects, characters, figures, or colors used to represent abstract ideas or concepts.*

### Orlando's Poems

The poems that Orlando nails to the trees of Ardenne are a testament to his love for Rosalind. In comparing her to the romantic heroines of classical literature—Helen, Cleopatra, Lucretia—Orlando takes his place among a long line of poets who regard the love object as a bit of earthbound perfection. Much to the amusement of Rosalind, Celia, and Touchstone, Orlando's efforts are far less accomplished than, say, Ovid's, and so bring into sharp focus the silliness of which all lovers are guilty. Orlando's "tedious homil[ies] of love" stand as a reminder of the wide gap that exists between the fancies of literature and the kind of love that exists in the real world (III.ii.143).

### THE SLAIN DEER

In Act IV, scene ii, Jaques and other lords in Duke Senior's party kill a deer. Jaques proposes to "set the deer's horns upon [the hunter's] head for a branch of victory" (IV.ii.4–5). To an Elizabethan audience, however, the slain deer would have signaled more than just an accomplished archer. As the song that follows the lord's return to camp makes clear, the deer placed atop the hunter's head is a symbol of cuckoldry, commonly represented by a man with horns atop his head. Allusions to the cuckolded man run throughout the play, betraying one of the dominant anxieties of the age—that women are sexually uncontrollable—and pointing out the schism between ideal and imperfect love.

### GANYMEDE

Rosalind's choice of alternative identities is significant. Ganymede is the cupbearer and beloved of Jove and is a standard symbol of homosexual love. In the context of the play, her choice of an alter ego contributes to a continuum of sexual possibilities.

# SUMMARY & ANALYSIS

## ACT I, SCENE I

### SUMMARY

Orlando, the youngest son of the recently deceased Sir Rowland de Bois, describes his unfortunate state of affairs to Adam, Sir Rowland's loyal former servant. Upon his father's death, Orlando was bequeathed a mere 1,000 crowns, a paltry sum for a young man of his social background. His only hope for advancement is if his brother, Oliver, honors their father's wish and provides him with a decent education. Oliver, as the eldest son, inherited virtually everything in his father's estate, yet he not only neglects this charge but actively disobeys it. Although he arranges for his other brother, Jaques, to attend school, Oliver refuses to allow Orlando any education whatsoever, leaving the young man to lament that his upbringing is little different from the treatment of a piece of livestock. Orlando has long borne this ill treatment, but he admits to Adam that he feels rising within himself a great resentment against his servile condition and vows that he will no longer endure it.

Oliver enters, and the hostility between the brothers soon boils over into violence. Orlando claims that the system that allows the eldest son to inherit the bulk of a father's estate does not reduce the ancestral blood in the other sons. Oliver, offended by his brother's insolence, assails Orlando, while Orlando seizes Oliver by the throat. Adam tries to intervene, seeking peace in the name of their father, but the brothers do not heed him. Orlando, undoubtedly the stronger of the two, refuses to unhand his brother until Oliver promises to treat him like a gentleman, or else give him his due portion of their father's estate so that he may pursue a gentlemanly lifestyle on his own. Oliver hastily agrees to give Orlando part of his small inheritance and, in a rage, dismisses Orlando and Adam, whom he chastises as an "old dog" (I.i.69).

Oliver bids his servant Denis to summon Charles, the court wrestler, who has been waiting to speak to him. Oliver asks Charles for the news at court, and Charles reports that Duke Senior has been usurped by his younger brother, Duke Frederick, and has fled with a number of loyal lords to the Forest of Ardenne. Because the noblemen have forfeited their land and wealth by going into voluntary exile, Duke Frederick allows them to wander unmolested. When Oliver asks if Senior's daughter, Rosalind, has been banished, Charles says that the girl remains at court. Not only does Duke Frederick love Rosalind as though she is his own daughter, but the duke's daughter, Celia, has a great friendship with her cousin and cannot bear to be parted from her. Charles asserts that two ladies never loved as Celia and Rosalind do. Charles then admits his real reason for coming to see Oliver: he has heard rumors that Orlando plans to disguise himself in order to enter a wrestling match at the royal court. Because Charles's reputation depends upon the brutal defeat of all of his opponents, he worries that he will harm Orlando. He begs Oliver to intervene on his brother's behalf, but Oliver replies that Orlando is a conniving and deceitful scoundrel. He convinces Charles that Orlando will use poison or some other trick in order to bring down the wrestler. Charles threatens to repay Orlando in kind, and Oliver, pleased with Charles's promise, plots a way to deliver his brother to the wrestling ring.

### ANALYSIS

Shakespeare begins his play with a pair of dueling brothers, an amendment of his source material—Thomas Lodge's popular prose romance, *Rosalynde*—that allows him to establish, with great economy, the corrupt nature of so-called civilized life. Oliver's mistreatment of his brother spurs Orlando to journey into the curative Forest of Ardenne as surely as Frederick's actions did his own brother Duke Senior, which immediately locates the play in the pastoral tradition: those wounded by life at court seek the restorative powers of the country. But fraternal hostilities are also deeply biblical and resonate with the story of Cain's murder of Abel, an act that confirmed mankind's delivery from paradise into a world of malignity and harm. The injustice of Oliver's refusal to educate or otherwise share his fortune with Orlando seems all the more outrageous because it is perfectly legal. The practice of primogeniture stipulated that the eldest son inherits the whole of his father's estate so that estates would not fragment into smaller parcels. Primogeniture was not mandated by law in Shakespeare's England, but it was a firmly entrenched part of traditional English custom. With such a system governing society, inequality, greed, and animosity become unfortunate inevitabilities, and many younger sons in Shakespeare's time would have shared Orlando's resentment.

In this opening scene, Shakespeare begins to muse on another theme common in pastoral literature: the origins of gentleness. As scholar Jean E. Howard makes clear in her introduction to the play, "gentleness" refers to both nobility and a virtuous nature (p. 1591). Elizabethans were supremely interested in whether this quality could be achieved or whether one had to be born with it, and Orlando shows himself to be a man of the times. Though Oliver has denied him all forms of education and noble living, Orlando nonetheless has a desire for gentleness. As he assails Oliver, he claims that his "gentleman-like qualities" have been obscured, but feels confident that he could develop them still (I.i.59). Of course, Oliver's behavior suggests that gentleness has little to do with being born into nobility. Though he has the vast majority of his father's estate at his fingertips, he proves lacking in the generosity and grace that would make him a true gentleman. The audience, then, looks optimistically to Orlando, who vows to go find his fortune on his own.

The episode with the wrestler Charles is important for several reasons. First, it provides further evidence of the prejudices that rule court society. Charles visits Oliver because he worries about defeating Orlando. Although Charles is paid to be a brute, he fears that pummeling a nobleman, even one so bereft of fortune as Orlando, may win him disfavor in the court. Such deference on Charles's part speaks to the severe hierarchy of power that structures court life. Charles also provides necessary plot explication. Through Charles's report to Oliver, Shakespeare sketches the backdrop of his comedy: the usurpation of Duke Senior by Duke Frederick, Rosalind's precarious situation, and the qualities of life in the Forest of Ardenne. Although set in France, the forest to which Duke Senior and his loyal lords flee is intentionally reminiscent of Sherwood Forest, the home of Robin Hood. It is, in Charles's estimation, a remnant of "the golden world," a time of ease and abundance from which the modern world has fallen (I.i.103). Thus, before we ever see Ardenne, which cannot be located on any map, we understand it as a place where Orlando will find the remedy he so desperately seeks.

## ACT I, SCENES II–III

### SUMMARY: ACT I, SCENE II

Rosalind is depressed over the banishment of her father, Duke Senior. Her cousin, Celia, attempts to cheer her up. Celia promises that as the sole heir of the usurping Duke Frederick, she will give the throne to Rosalind upon his death. In gratitude, Rosalind promises to be less melancholy, and the two women wittily discuss the roles of "Fortune" and "Nature" in determining the circumstances of one's life (I.ii.26–47). They are interrupted by the court jester, Touchstone, who mockingly tells of a knight without honor who still swore by it. Le Beau, a dapper young courtier, also arrives and intrigues them with the promise of a wrestling match featuring the phenomenal strength and skill of the wrestler Charles.

The match's participants enter with many members of the court, including Duke Frederick, who cordially greets Rosalind and Celia. The duke remarks on the danger Charles's young challenger faces, and he suggests that the girls attempt to dissuade the present challenger from his effort to defeat the wrestler. Rosalind and Celia agree and call to the young man, who turns out to be Orlando. Try as they might, they cannot sway him. He remains deaf to their pleas and speaks as if he has absolutely nothing to lose. Orlando and Charles wrestle, and Orlando quickly defeats his opponent. Amazed, Duke Frederick asks Orlando to reveal his identity. When Orlando responds that he is the youngest son of Sir Rowland de Bois, the duke laments that he wishes Orlando had been someone else's son, admitting that he and Sir Rowland were enemies. Rosalind and Celia rush in to offer their congratulations, and Rosalind admits how deeply her father admired Orlando's father. In the exchange, Orlando and Rosalind become mutually smitten, though both are too tongue-tied to confess their feelings.

Immediately after Rosalind and Celia take their leave, Le Beau warns Orlando that, though his victory and conduct deserve great praise, he will get none from Duke Frederick. In fact, La Beau says, the duke is due for a dangerous outburst. Orlando, already heartsick over Rosalind, resolves to flee from the tyrannical duke.

### Summary: Act I, scene iii

Rosalind is overcome with her emotions for Orlando. Celia asks her cousin how she could possibly manage to fall in love with Orlando so quickly. Just then, Duke Frederick approaches and demands that Rosalind leave the royal court. He denounces her as a traitor and threatens her with death should she be found within twenty miles of court. Rosalind does not know how she has offended the duke and pleads her innocence, but the duke remains firm. When Rosalind asks him to explain his decision to banish her, Duke Frederick replies that she is her father's daughter, and that is enough. Celia makes an impassioned plea on Rosalind's behalf, but the duke condemns Rosalind for her "smoothness" and "silence," and tries to convince his daughter that she will seem more beautiful and virtuous after Rosalind is gone (I.iii.71–72). Celia announces that in banishing Rosalind, Duke Frederick has also banished Celia, and the two women decide to seek out Duke Senior in the Forest of Ardenne. Realizing that such a journey would be incredibly dangerous for two wealthy, attractive young women, they decide to travel in disguise: Celia as a common shepherdess and Rosalind as a young man. Celia renames herself Alicna, while Rosalind dubs her disguised self Ganymede, after the cupbearer to Jove. The two decide to convince Touchstone, a clown, to accompany them on their journey.

---

ANALYSIS: ACT I, SCENES II–III

As many critics have pointed out, Rosalind's relationship with Celia suggests an element of homoeroticism. Homoeroticism differs from homosexuality in connoting feelings of desire or longing between members of the same sex, but not necessarily the desire for actual sex acts. Celia begins Act I, scene ii by challenging the depth of her cousin's love for her, claiming that the depressed Rosalind would be content if she only returned Celia's love. Celia's language here conforms to conventional protestations of romantic love, and there is no doubt that the women's friendship is remarkable. When Celia pleads with Duke Frederick to allow Rosalind to stay at court, she points out that the pair has always slept in the same bed—people normally slept two to a bed in Shakespeare's time—and went everywhere together, "coupled and inseparable" (I.iii.70). The women's special bond is not lost on those who witness their friendship—as Duke Frederick's courtier, Le Beau, exclaims, the cousins share a love that is "dearer than the natural bond of sisters" (I.ii.243).

Before jumping to conclusions about the nature of Rosalind and Celia's relationship, it is important to note that contemporary ideas about sexuality are quite different from Elizabethan ideas. Whereas people today tend to expect adherence to neatly defined and mutually exclusive categories of behavior, such as heterosexuality or homosexuality, sexual identity was more loosely defined in Shakespeare's England. Then, in literature and culture, if not in actual practice, Elizabethans were tolerant of same-sex couplings—indeed, homosexuality was an inescapable part of the Greek and Roman classics that made up an educated person's culture in

Shakespeare's day. At the same time, Elizabethans could be very inflexible in their notions of the sexual and social roles that different genders play. They placed greater importance than we do on the external markers of gender such as clothing and behavior; so to Elizabethans, Rosalind's decision to masquerade as a man may have been more thrilling than her homoerotic bond with Celia and perhaps even threatening to the social order. By assuming the clothes and likeness of a man, Rosalind treats herself to powers that are normally beyond her reach as a woman. For instance, instead of waiting to be wooed, she adopts the freedom to court a lover of her choosing. By subverting something as simple as a dress code, Rosalind ends up transgressing the Elizabethans' carefully monitored boundaries of gender and social power.

Indeed, it is this very freedom that Rosalind seeks as she departs for the Forest of Ardenne: "Now go we in content, / To liberty, and not to banishment" (I.iii.131–132). By christening herself Ganymede, Rosalind underscores the liberation that awaits her in the woods. Ganymede is the name of Jove's beautiful young male page and lover, and the name is borrowed in other works of literature and applied to beautiful young homosexuals. But while the name links Rosalind to a long tradition of homosexuals in literature, it does not necessarily confine her to an exclusively homosexual identity. To view Rosalind as a lesbian who settles for a socially sanctifying marriage with Orlando, or to view Celia as her jilted lover, is to relegate both of them to the unpleasantly restrictive quarters of contemporary sexual politics. The Forest of Ardenne is big enough to embrace both homosexual and heterosexual desires—it allows for both, for all, rather than either/or.

## ACT II, SCENES I–IV

### SUMMARY: ACT II, SCENE I

> [O]ur life, exempt from public haunt,
> Finds tongues in trees, books in the running brooks,
> Sermons in stones, and good in everything.
>
> (See QUOTATIONS, p. 46)

The banished Duke Senior expounds on the wonders of life in the forest. He tells his associates that he prefers forest dwelling to the "painted pomp" of courtly existence (II.i.3). He reminds them that their existence in Ardenne is free from danger and that their greatest worry here is nothing worse than the cold winter wind. The woods provide Duke Senior with everything he needs, from conversation to education to spiritual edification, for he "[f]inds tongues in trees, books in the running brooks, / Sermons in stones, and good in everything" (II.i.16–17). Lord Amiens agrees with him. The duke suggests that they hunt some venison, but he cannot help but mourn the fate of the deer, who, though natives of Ardenne, are violently slaughtered. One lord announces that the melancholy lord Jaques has seconded this observation, declaring Senior guiltier of usurpation than his loveless brother, Duke Frederick. Duke Senior, in good humor, asks one of his men to bring him to Jaques, because arguing with him is such fun.

### Summary: Act II, scene ii

Back at court, Duke Frederick is enraged to discover the disappearances of Celia, Rosalind, and Touchstone; he cannot believe that the three could leave court without anyone's notice. One attending lord reports that Celia's gentlewoman overheard Celia and Rosalind complimenting Orlando, and she speculates that wherever the women are, Orlando is likely with them. Frederick seizes on this information and commands that Oliver be recruited to find his brother.

### Summary: Act II, scene iii

Orlando returns to his former home, where the servant Adam greets him. News of the young man's victory over Charles precedes him, and Adam worries that Orlando's strength and bravery will be the keys to his downfall. Adam begs Orlando not to enter Oliver's house. Oliver, he reports, having learned of Orlando's triumph, plans to burn the place where Orlando sleeps in hopes of destroying Orlando with it. "Abhor it," Adam warns, "fear it, do not enter it" (II.iii.29). Orlando wonders about his fate, speculating that without a home, he may be destined to eke out a living as a common highway robber. Adam suggests that the two of them take to the road with his modest life's savings. Touched by Adam's constant service, Orlando agrees.

### Summary: Act II, scene iv

Rosalind, Celia, and Touchstone arrive, safe but exhausted, in the Forest of Ardenne. The three sit down to rest, but before long they are interrupted by two shepherds: old Corin and young Silvius. The shepherds are so wrapped up in their conversation about Silvius's hopeless love and devotion to the shepherdess Phoebe that they do not notice the three travelers. Corin, who claims to have loved a thousand times, tries to advise Silvius, but the young man, maintaining that his companion could not possibly understand the depth of his feelings, wanders off. Rosalind, Celia, and Touchstone approach Corin and ask where they might find a place to rest. When Corin admits that his master's modest holdings are up for sale, Rosalind and Celia decide to buy the property.

---

### ANALYSIS: ACT II, SCENES I–IV

Pastoral literature makes a clear distinction between the quality of life and benefits of living in the city versus the country. The stresses of the former, this genre romantically suggests, may be healed by the charms of the latter; thus Act II introduces us to the Forest of Ardenne after we witness characters undergo banishment from courtly life. Although supposedly situated in France, Shakespeare's forest bears closer resemblance to the fantastical getaway of *A Midsummer Night's Dream* than to any identifiable geography. It may not be overrun with mischievous fairies and sprites, but it serves the function of correcting what has gone wrong with the everyday world. However, even with that purpose in mind, Ardenne is no Eden. Though Duke Frederick praises the forest as preferable to the artificial ceremony of the court, he takes care to describe its hardships. With its wild animals and erratic weather, Ardenne can hardly be called a paradise, and at the same time the duke celebrates Ardenne, he also draws attention to the difference between that forest and Eden or the Golden Age.

The forest is a lovely but ultimately temporary haven for the characters who seek refuge from exile. One reason for the transience of this sanctuary is that the city dwellers are, by the play's end, ready to return to court. Jaques, a stock character who represents the melancholy brooder, suggests a more troubling reason for the temporary nature of the forest's pristine state and restorative powers. Man, he suggests, will sooner or later mar the forest's beauty. Grieved by the killing of the deer, Jaques claims that Duke Senior is guiltier of usurpation than his crown-robbing brother, Duke Frederick. According to Jaques, wherever men go, they bring with them the possibility of the very perils that make life in the "envious court" so unbearable (II.i.4). None of Duke Senior's courtiers disagrees with Jaques, but the melancholy lord's criticism lacks real sting. Indeed, Duke Senior sees Jaques as little more than entertainment, for the extremity of Jaques's mood prompts Senior to declare amusingly, "I love to cope him in these sullen fits, / For then he's full of matter"—matter being the word for pus in Shakespearean English (II.i.67–68). In a play that celebrates the complexity and the range of human emotions, there is little room for someone like Jaques, who knows how to sing only one tune.

With the introduction of Silvius, *As You Like It* begins to explore the foolishness of love as opposed to its delightfulness. Unlike Rosalind, who is equipped with enough wit to recognize the silliness of her sudden devotion to Orlando, Silvius is powerless in his attraction to Phoebe. In his laments to Corin in Act II, scene iv, he presents himself as love's only true victim, and he implies that no one has ever loved as he loves Phoebe. Although Rosalind at first pities the shepherd's predicament as curiously close to her own, she soon enough comes to share Touchstone's observation on the necessary foolishness of being in love. As he watches Silvius call out to the absent Phoebe, Touchstone says, "We that are true lovers run into strange capers. But as all is mortal in nature, so is all nature in love mortal in folly" (II.iv.47–49). Touchstone's inarticulate and rude manner of speaking makes him a true touchstone for Rosalind, bringing into greater relief her supreme eloquence and wit. Here, however, he utters two essential pieces of truth: everything in the natural world is temporary, and every lover naturally behaves like a fool. But the fact that so many characters fall in love in Ardenne proves that they are less love's victims than its willing subjects.

## ACT II, SCENES V–VII

### SUMMARY: ACT II, SCENE V
As Amiens strolls through the Forest of Ardenne with Jaques in tow, he sings a song inviting his listeners to lie with him "[u]nder the greenwood tree" (II.v.1), where there are no enemies but "winter and rough weather" (II.v.8). Jaques begs him to continue, but Amiens hesitates, claiming that the song will only make Jaques melancholy. The warning does not deter Jaques, who proudly claims that he can "suck melancholy out of a song as a weasel sucks eggs" (II.v.11–12). While the other lords in attendance prepare for Duke Senior's meal, Amiens leads them in finishing the song. Jaques follows with a verse set to the same tune, which he himself wrote. In it, he chides those foolish enough to leave their wealth and leisure for life in the forest. Amiens leaves to summon the duke to dinner.

## SUMMARY: ACT II, SCENE VI

Orlando and Adam enter the Forest of Ardenne. Adam is exhausted from travel and claims that he will soon die from hunger. Orlando assures his loyal servant that he will find him food. Before he sets off to hunt, Orlando fears leaving Adam lying in "the bleak air" and carries him off to shelter (II.vi.12).

## SUMMARY: ACT II, SCENE VII

> *And so from hour to hour we ripe and ripe,*
> *And then from hour to hour we rot and rot;*
> *And thereby hangs a tale.*

> *(See* QUOTATIONS, *p. 47)*

Duke Senior returns to camp to find that Jaques has disappeared. When a lord reports that Jaques has last been seen in good spirits, the duke worries that happiness in one who is typically so miserable portends discord in the universe. Just after the duke commands the lord to find Jaques, Jaques appears. He is uncharacteristically merry and explains that while wandering through the forest, he met a fool. He repeats the fool's witty observations about Lady Fortune and proclaims that he himself would like to be a fool. In this position, Jaques reasons, he would be able to speak his mind freely, thereby cleansing "the foul body of th'infected world" with the "medicine" of his criticism (II.vii.60–61). The duke laments the sin of "chiding sin" and reminds Jaques that he himself is guilty of many of the evils he would inevitably criticize in others (II.v.64). Their playful argument is interrupted when Orlando barges onto the scene, drawing his sword and demanding food. The duke asks whether Orlando's rudeness is a function of distress or bad breeding and, once Orlando has regained his composure, invites him to partake of the banquet. Orlando goes off to fetch Adam. Duke Senior observes that he and his men are far from alone in their unhappiness: there is much strife in the world. Jaques replies that the world is a stage and "all the men and women merely players" (II.vii.139). All humans pass through the stages of infancy, childhood, and adulthood; they experience love and seek honor, but all eventually succumb to the debility of old age and "mere oblivion" (II.vii.164). Orlando returns with Adam and all begin to eat. The duke soon realizes that Orlando is the son of Sir Rowland, the duke's old friend, and heartily welcomes the young man.

## ANALYSIS: ACT II, SCENES V–VII

Both Act II, scene v and Act II, scene vi deal primarily with the melancholy lord, Jaques, who offers a sullen perspective on the otherwise comedic events in Ardenne. He turns Amiens's song about the pleasures of leisurely life into a means of berating the foresters, and he comes close to playing the part of the fool, in the sense that he turns a critical eye on a world in which he lives but does not fully inhabit. But unlike Feste in *Twelfth Night* or the fool in *King Lear*, Jaques does not demonstrate the insight or wisdom that would make his observations truly arresting or illuminating. His most impressive speech in the play begins with a familiar set piece in Elizabethan drama: "All the world's a stage, / And all the men and women merely players" (II.vii.138–139). He goes on to describe the seven stages of a man's life, from infancy to death, through his roles as lover and soldier, but Jaques's observations may strike us as untrue or banal. His estimation that lovers sigh "like furnace, with a woeful ballad / Made to his mistress' eyebrow" is humorous, and it certainly describes the kind of intemperate, undiscriminating affection that Silvius shows to Phoebe, or Phoebe to Ganymede (II.vii.147–148). But the criticism seems ill-suited to a play as aware and forgiving of love's silliness as *As You Like It*. As a philosopher, Jaques falls short of accurately describing the complexity of Rosalind's feelings for Orlando; his musings bear the narrow and pinched shortcomings of the habitually sullen.

Jaques's sullenness blinds him to his own foolishness regarding life. Jaques goes on to describe man's later years, the decline into second childhood and obliviousness, without teeth, eyesight, taste, or anything else. Countering Jaques's unflattering picture of old age, Orlando carries Adam to the duke's banquet table, the old man entering his final years with his loyalty, generosity of spirit, and appetite intact. Although the thought of serving as Duke Frederick's fool appeals to him, Jaques ultimately lacks the wit, wisdom, and heart to perform the task. When he meets Touchstone in the forest, he sings the clown's praises, quoting with glee Touchstone's nihilistic musings on the passage of time: "And so from hour to hour we ripe and ripe, / And then from hour to hour we rot and rot" (II.vii.26–27). Jaques does not realize that Touchstone's "deep-contemplative" speech is a bawdy mockery of his own brooding behavior (II.vii.31). Indeed, throughout the play, Jaques remains so mired in his own moodiness that he sees very little of the world he so desperately wants to criticize. Knowing that Jaques's eyes are trained on men's baser instincts, the duke doubts Jaques's ability to serve as a proper and entertaining fool. Jaques, he feels, would be a boor, berating the courtiers for sins that Jaques himself has committed. This exchange points to an important difference between Jaques and the duke: the former is committed to being unhappy in the world and will suffer in it, while the latter is happy to make the best of the world he is given and will thrive, as the title of the play seems to promise.

## ACT III, SCENES I–II

### SUMMARY: ACT III, SCENE I
Oliver, who has been unable to locate Orlando, reports to Duke Frederick at court. The duke chastises him for his failure and commands him to find Orlando within a year's time or else forfeit the whole of his property. Frederick turns Oliver out to search for Orlando and seizes his lands and worldly goods until Orlando is delivered to court.

### SUMMARY: ACT III, SCENE II
Orlando runs through the Forest of Ardenne, mad with love. He hangs poems that he has composed in Rosalind's honor on every tree, hoping that passersby will see her "virtue witnessed everywhere" (III.ii.8). Corin and Touchstone enter, but are too engrossed in a conversation about the relative merits of court and country life to pay attention to Orlando's verses. Corin argues that polite manners at court are of no consequence in the country. Touchstone asks him to provide evidence to support this thesis and then challenges the shepherd's reasoning.

Rosalind enters, disguised as Ganymede. She reads one of Orlando's poems, which compares her to a priceless jewel. Touchstone mocks the verse, claiming that he could easily churn out a comparable succession of rhymes. He does so with couplets that liken Rosalind to a cat in heat, a thorny rose, and a prostitute who is transported to the pillory on a cart. Rosalind rebukes Touchstone for his meddling. Just then, Celia enters disguised as the shepherdess Aliena. She, too, has found one of Orlando's verses and reads it aloud. The women agree that the verses are terribly written, yet Rosalind is eager to learn the identity of their author. Celia teases her friend, hesitating to reveal this secret until Rosalind is nearly insane with anticipation. When Celia admits that Orlando has penned the poems, Rosalind can hardly believe it. Like a smitten schoolgirl, she asks a dozen questions about her intended lover, wanting to know everything from where he is to what he looks like.

As Celia does her best to answer these questions, despite Rosalind's incessant interruptions, Orlando and Jaques enter. Hiding, the women eavesdrop on their conversation. Orlando and Jaques clearly do not care for one another's company and exchange a series of barbed insults. Jaques dislikes Orlando's sentimental love, declaring it the worst possible fault, while Orlando scoffs at Jaques's melancholy. Eager to part, Jaques walks off into the forest, leaving Orlando alone. Rosalind decides to confront Orlando. She approaches him as the young man Ganymede, and speaks of a man that has been carving the name Rosalind on the trees. Orlando insists that he is the man so "love-shaked" and begs her for a "remedy" (III.ii.332–333). She claims to recognize the symptoms of those who have fallen under the spell of true love, and assures Orlando that he exhibits none of them. He is, she says, too neatly dressed to be madly in love. She promises to cure him if he promises to woo Ganymede as though Ganymede were Rosalind. As Ganymede, Rosalind vows to make the very idea of love unappealing to Orlando by acting the part of a fickle lover. Orlando is quite sure he is beyond cure, but Rosalind says, "I would cure you if you would but call me Rosalind and come every day to my cot, and woo me" (III.ii.381–382). With all his heart, Orlando agrees.

### Analysis: Act III, scenes i–ii

In Act III, as the play moves from Duke Frederick's court into the Forest of Ardenne, Shakespeare explores more fully the complexities of his major themes: the merits of country versus city life, and the delights and dismays of romantic love. The conversation between Touchstone and Corin in Act III, scene ii provides interesting insight into the matter of city versus country living. Although Corin concedes the argument to Touchstone, calling the clown's high but hollow rhetoric "too courtly . . . for me," we note that Corin's speech is much clearer and his logic more sound than Touchstone's (III.ii.61). Corin's declaration that "[t]hose that are good manners at the court are as ridiculous in the country as the behaviour of the country is most mockable at the court" is not only sensible, it is also in keeping with the guiding philosophy of the play: that the world is full of contradictions that do not cancel one another out, but exist side by side (III.ii.40–42). Corin's willingness to rest, then, is not so much an admission of defeat as a recognition that court *and* country, along with the style *and* the substance that they respectively represent, must coexist.

As the argument between Touchstone and Corin plays out, we witness the repercussions of Orlando's lovesickness. When characters fall in love in *As You Like It,* they invariably fall hard and fast, abandoning all reason in their desperate attempts to win the object of desire. Orlando is no exception, as the silly and unskilled poems he tacks on the trees make clear. Here, Orlando's behavior accords with the Petrarchan model of romantic love (Petrarch is a fourteenth-century Italian poet whose lyrics elevate the woman he loves to an unattainable, semidivine status). Orlando's behavior leads him to great folly and prompts Jaques's sour declaration: "The worst fault you have is to be in love" (III.ii.258). But, sour though it is, the sentiment is not Orlando's alone. As Rosalind reads Orlando's verses, she comments on their poor composition, but this shortcoming does not stop her from enjoying them. It is much to the play's credit that it conceives of such irrational devotion as both a virtue and a vice. It is also the greatest testament of the depth of Rosalind's character: only she is capacious and generous enough to welcome and thrive on such contradictions.

The play also adds an interesting twist on the stage convention of cross-dressing as Rosalind decides to use her disguise as Ganymede, in effect, to woo Orlando. The erotic possibilities here are nearly endless, considering that Rosalind dresses as a rather effeminate man and offers to provide Orlando with love lessons so that Orlando may win his beloved Rosalind. The complexities of the situation multiply when we consider that in Shakespeare's era, Rosalind would have been played by a boy actor. As the audience watches a boy playing a woman who plays a man in order to win a man's love, the neat borders of gender and sexuality become hopelessly muddled.

## ACT III, SCENES III–V

### SUMMARY: ACT III, SCENE III

Touchstone and a goatherd named Audrey wander through the forest, while Jaques follows behind them, eavesdropping. Touchstone laments that the gods have not made Audrey "poetical" (III.iii.12). Were she a lover of poetry, she would appreciate the falsehoods of which all lovers are guilty and would be dishonest, a quality that Touchstone prefers she possess. His reason behind encouraging her dishonesty is that to have beauty *and* honesty together, as he claims he does in Audrey, is "to have honey a sauce to sugar" (III.iii.25). Nevertheless, Touchstone has arranged to marry Audrey in the forest with Sir Oliver Martext, a vicar from a nearby village, officiating. Touchstone determines that many wives cheat on their husbands, but claims that the horns of cuckoldry are nothing of which to be ashamed. Oliver Martext arrives to perform the wedding ceremony and insists that someone "give the woman" so that the ceremony is "lawful" (III.iii.55–58). Jaques offers his services but convinces Touchstone that he should marry in a proper church. The clown counters that a nonchurch wedding will make for an ill marriage and that an ill marriage will make it easier for him to abandon his wife, but in the end he acquiesces. Jaques, Touchstone, and Audrey leave the rather bewildered vicar alone in the forest.

## SUMMARY: ACT III, SCENE IV

Orlando has failed to show up for his morning appointment with Ganymede, the disguised Rosalind, and she is distraught. She wants desperately to weep. Rosalind compares Orlando's hair to that of the infamous betrayer of Christ, Judas. Celia insists that Orlando's hair is browner than Judas's, and Rosalind agrees, slowly convincing herself that her lover is no traitor. Celia, however, then suggests that in matters of love, there is little truth in Orlando. A lover's oath, Celia reasons, is of no more account than that of a bartender.

Corin enters and interrupts the women's conversation. He explains that the young shepherd, Silvius, whose complaints about the tribulations of love Rosalind and Celia witness earlier, has decided to woo and win Phoebe. Corin invites the women to see the "pageant" of a hopeless lover and the scornful object of his desire, and Rosalind heads off to see the scene play out (III.iv.46). Indeed, she determines to do more than watch—she plans to intervene in the affair.

## SUMMARY: ACT III, SCENE V

Silvius has confessed his love to Phoebe, but his words fall on hostile ears. As the scene opens, he pleads with her not to reject him so bitterly, lest she prove worse than the "common executioner," who has enough decency to ask forgiveness of those he kills (III.v.3). Rosalind and Celia, both still disguised, enter along with Corin to watch Phoebe's cruel response. Phoebe mocks Silvius's hyperbolic language, asking why he fails to fall down if her eyes are the murderers he claims them to be. Silvius assures her that the wounds of love are invisible, but Phoebe insists that the shepherd not approach her again until she too can feel these invisible wounds. Rosalind steps out from her hiding place and begins to berate Phoebe, proclaiming that the shepherdess is no great beauty and should consider herself lucky to win Silvius's love. Confronted by what appears to be a handsome young man who treats her as harshly as she treats Silvius, Phoebe instantly falls in love with Ganymede. Rosalind, realizing this infatuation, mocks Phoebe further. Rosalind and Celia depart, and Phoebe employs Silvius, who can talk so well of love, to help her pursue Ganymede. Phoebe claims that she does not love Ganymede and wonders why she failed to defend herself against such criticism. She determines to write him "a very taunting letter," and orders Silvius to deliver it (III.v.135).

---

## ANALYSIS: ACT III, SCENES III–V

Although we learn of the romance between Audrey and Touchstone rather late in the game, the relationship is important to the play for many reasons. First, it produces laughs because of the incongruities between the two lovers. Touchstone delights in words and verbiage. He obsesses over them, wrings multiple—and often bawdy—meanings from them, and usually ends up tangling himself and others in them. That he chooses to wed Audrey, a simple goatherd who fails to comprehend the most basic vocabulary—the words "features," "poetical," and "foul" are all beyond her grasp—ensures the laughable absurdity of their exchange (III.iii.4, 13–14, 31). Indeed, the play offers few moments more outrageous than Audrey's declaration of virtue: "I am not a slut, though I thank the gods I am foul" (III.iii.31).

The rustic romance between Audrey and Touchstone also provides a pointed contrast with the flowery, verbose love of Silvius for Phoebe or Orlando for Rosalind. Whereas Phoebe and Silvius are caught up in the poetics of love—with the man in agonizing pursuit of an unattainable but, to his mind, perfect lover—the attraction between Touchstone and Audrey is far from idealized. Indeed, if Audrey cannot grasp the meaning of the word "poetical," there is little hope that she will be able to fulfill the part dictated to her by literary convention. Ideals have little to do with Touchstone's affections for Audrey. By his own admission, the clown's passions are much easier to understand. In explaining to Jaques his decision to marry Audrey, Touchstone says, "As the ox hath his bow, sir, the horse his curb, and the falcon her bells, so man hath his desires" (III.iii.66–67). Here, Touchstone equates his sexual desire to various restraining devices for animals. Sexual gratification, or "nibbling," to use Touchstone's phrase, will keep his otherwise untamed passions in check (III.iii.68).

Although Silvius and Phoebe's and Touchstone and Audrey's are two very different kinds of love relationships, taken together they form a complete satire of the two major influences on the play—pastoralism and courtly love. In pastoral literature, city dwellers take to the country in order to commune with and learn valuable lessons from its inhabitants. Audrey represents a truly rural individual, uncorrupted by the politics of court life, but she is, in all respects, far from ideal. In her supreme want of intelligence, Audrey shows the absurd unreality of the pastoral ideal of eloquent shepherds and shepherdesses. Silvius aspires to such eloquence and nearly achieves it, and his poetic plea for Phoebe's mercy conforms to the conventions of the distraught but always lyrically precise lover. But Phoebe exposes the absurdity of Silvius's lines by dragging romance into the harsh, unforgiving light of reality. When taken literally, his insistence that his lover's eyes are his "executioner" (III.v.3) seems hopelessly lame when Phoebe demands, "Now show the wound mine eye hath made in thee" (III.v.20).

If Audrey and Touchstone's and Phoebe and Silvius's relationships stand at opposite ends of the romance continuum, then Rosalind, in her courtship of Orlando, struggles to find a more livable middle ground. Although Phoebe wisely points out the literal flaws in Silvius's verse, she cannot help falling into the same trap herself regarding Ganymede. In the entire play, only Rosalind can appreciate *both* the ideal and the real. Although she possesses the unflinching vision required to chastise Phoebe for her cruelty and Silvius for his blindness to it, she cannot help but indulge in the absurdity of romantic love, allowing herself to have a fit over Orlando's tardiness. This inconsistency may explain why Rosalind is such a seductive, winning character: in her ability to experience and appreciate all emotions, she appeals to everyone.

# ACT IV, SCENES I–II

## SUMMARY: ACT IV, SCENE I

> Men have died from time to time, and worms have eaten
> them, but not for love.
>
> (See QUOTATIONS, p. 47)

Jaques approaches Rosalind, who is still in her disguise as
Ganymede, wishing to become better acquainted. Rosalind criticizes Jaques for the extremity of his melancholy. When Jaques
claims that "'tis good to be sad and say nothing," Rosalind compares such activity to being "a post" (IV.i.8–9). Jaques defends himself, outlining for Rosalind the unique composition of his sadness,
but Rosalind gets the better of him and he departs.

Orlando arrives an hour late for his lesson in love. As agreed, he
addresses Ganymede as if the young man were his beloved Rosalind
and asks her to forgive his tardiness. Rosalind refuses, insisting that
a true lover could not bear to squander "a part of the thousand part
of a minute in the affairs of love" (IV.i.40–41). She goes on to suggest that Orlando's love is worse than a snail's, for though a snail
comes slowly, he carries his house on his back. Eventually, though,
Rosalind relents and invites Orlando to woo her. The lesson begins:
when he says that he desires to kiss her before speaking, she suggests
that he save his kiss for the moment when conversation lags. What,
Orlando worries, should he do if his kiss is denied? Rosalind reas-
sures him that a denied kiss would only give him "new matter" to
discuss with his lover (IV.i.69–70). When Rosalind refuses his affections, Orlando claims he will die. She responds that, despite the
poet's romantic imagination, no man in the entire history of the
world has died from a love-related cause.

Rosalind then changes her mood, assuming a "more coming-on
disposition" (IV.i.96). She accepts and returns Orlando's declarations of love and urges Celia to play the part of a priest and marry
them. Rosalind reminds Orlando that women often become dis-
agreeable after marriage, but Orlando does not believe this truism
of his love. He begs leave in order to dine with Duke Senior, promising to return within two hours. Rosalind teasingly chastises him for
parting with her but warns him not to be a minute late in keeping his
promise. After Orlando departs, Celia berates Rosalind for so badly
characterizing the female sex. Rosalind responds by exclaiming

how vast her love for Orlando has grown. Only Cupid, she says, can fathom the depth of her affection.

## SUMMARY: ACT IV, SCENE II

Jaques and some of Duke Senior's loyal followers kill a deer and decide to present it to the duke. They plan to set the animal's horns upon the hunter's head as a crown of victory. Jaques asks the men to sing a song that fits the occasion. They launch into a tune about cuckoldry, which is symbolized by a man with horns on his head. The song proclaims that cuckoldry is timeless and borne by all men, and thus it is not something of which to be ashamed.

---

## ANALYSIS: ACT IV, SCENES I–II

When Rosalind chastises Jaques for his oppressively melancholy ramblings, her words serve as a general criticism of the extremes to which the characters go in the play. Jaques admits that he is indeed the "melancholy fellow" of whom Rosalind has heard tell, and Rosalind upbraids him by saying, "Those that are in extremity of either [laughter or melancholy] are abominable fellows, and betray themselves to every modern censure worse than drunkards" (IV.i.3–7). Here, Rosalind speaks out not only against Jaques's willful sadness, but against the myriad excesses found around her. From Silvius's whimpering devotion to Phoebe's hauteur, to the crudely physical attraction of Audrey and Touchstone, to Jaques's melancholy, every type of extreme behavior in *As You Like It* is subject to mockery.

It is a testament to the clarity of Rosalind's vision that she does not spare herself or Orlando from this condemnation of extremes. When Orlando claims that he will die of love, Rosalind disproves him with one of the play's most famous and delightful speeches. Her insistence that literature has misrepresented and unduly romanticized the world's greatest lovers is a stringent antidote to Orlando's mewling, and supports Touchstone's earlier observation that "the truest poetry is the most feigning, and lovers are given to poetry; and what they swear in poetry it may be said, as lovers, they do feign" (III.iii.15–17). After dismantling Orlando's model of love, Rosalind goes on to assail the men who follow the model, claiming that the greatest romantics are transformed by marriage into inattentive, uncaring dictators. In addition to the jesting, there is a serious element of self-preservation in Rosalind's famous observation that "men are April when they woo, December when they wed"

(IV.i.124–125). When, on two occasions, Orlando is late for their appointment, Rosalind fears that her lover's devotion might not be steadfast, but she also *knows* that the thrill of romance is short-lived. Over time, love weathers and even dulls, an unhappy but inevitable truth that only Rosalind stops to consider: "the sky changes," she admits, "when [maids] are wives" (IV.i.126–127).

Rosalind might be construed as a spoilsport, out to ruin everyone else's fun by exposing the crumbling foundations of their love fantasies, but there is much more to her than this simplistic interpretation. Certainly, even her closest confidante Celia misunderstands her, claiming that Rosalind, in her attempts to drain the excess of Orlando's romanticism, has succeeded in disparaging the entire female sex. Rosalind's goal is less to represent the female gender than to show Orlando that, just as there is no such thing as a perfect and heroic love, there is also no such thing as an ideal and ideally worthy woman. By stripping Orlando and herself of the ideals that preoccupy him, Rosalind prepares them both for love in the real world, for a love that strikes a balance between the transcendent and the familiar, and for a love that blends the loftiness of Silvius's poetry with the baseness of Touchstone's desires. Thus, Rosalind's attacks on Orlando's idea of love are not an attack on love itself. After all, Rosalind herself is clearly and deeply in love. Her attempts to furnish Orlando with a more realistic understanding of love are a means of ensuring that their relationship will thrive in a world less enchanted than Ardenne.

## ACT IV, SCENE III

### SUMMARY

Rosalind and Celia, still in disguise, briefly discuss Orlando's tardiness. Two hours have passed, and he has not returned, as promised, to resume his love lessons. Silvius interrupts in order to deliver a letter to Ganymede. It is from Phoebe and, after he turns it over, Silvius warns the disguised Rosalind that its tone is harsh. Phoebe, he admits, looked very angry when she penned it. Rosalind scans the letter and reports that Phoebe judges Ganymede to be a young man without looks or manners. She then accuses Silvius of writing the letter himself, which he vehemently denies. Rosalind asserts that no woman could have written such a rude and defiant letter. To prove herself, she reads the letter aloud, but it turns out to be full of unabashedly romantic declarations, comparing Ganymede to a god who has destroyed Phoebe's heart. Baffled, Silvius asks if this language is what Ganymede calls chiding. Celia offers her pity to the shepherd, but Rosalind says he deserves none for loving such a woman as Phoebe. She sends Silvius back to Phoebe with the message that Ganymede will never love Phoebe unless Phoebe loves Silvius.

As Silvius leaves, Oliver enters. He asks for directions to Ganymede and Aliena's cottage. Then, looking over the pair, who are still in disguise, he asks if they are the brother and sister who own that property. When they admit that they are, Oliver remarks that his brother Orlando's description of the pair was very accurate. To Ganymede, Oliver delivers a bloody handkerchief on Orlando's behalf. Rosalind asks what has happened. Oliver tells a lengthy story: soon after leaving Ganymede, Orlando stumbled upon a ragged man asleep in the forest, who was being preyed upon by a "green and gilded snake" (IV.iii.107). Orlando succeeded in scaring the snake away, only to see a hungry lioness emerge from the underbrush. Orlando approached the ragged man, and recognized him as his brother. Orlando's first impulse was to let Oliver, who treated him so abominably, perish in the lion's jaws, but his nobler nature would not allow it. He fought off the lion, wounding his shoulder but ultimately saving Oliver's life. Orlando's kind and selfless gesture have transformed Oliver into a new man, and the elder brother confesses that he is ashamed of his former self. He continues, saying that he and Orlando made amends and went to see the duke. There, Orlando fainted, having lost a great deal of blood in his fight with the lioness. Before passing out completely, he charged Oliver to deliver an apology to Ganymede in the form of a bloodstained handkerchief. Upon hearing this story, Rosalind faints dead away. Celia and Oliver help her recover, and Oliver remarks that young Ganymede "lack[s] a man's heart" (IV.iii.163–164). Rosalind begs Oliver to impress upon Orlando how well she "counterfeited" a suitable reaction to his injury, in accordance with their lessons (IV.iii.167). Oliver protests that her reaction must be genuine, for her face is flushed. Rosalind, however, assures him that she was merely playing a part.

## ANALYSIS

In Act IV, scene iii, the play takes two important steps toward its resolution. First, Rosalind begins to tire of the game she plays. Her disguise as Ganymede allows her a number of freedoms that she could not enjoy as a woman: she can leave court, travel safely into the forest, express sexual desire, and initiate a romantic courtship. But her disguise also has its limitations. After all, it disables her from consummating her relationship with Orlando, and Rosalind does not relish the idea of acting out the indefinitely protracted desire depicted in Petrarch's love poetry. If Orlando were willing to test the bounds of their fiction and have sex with Ganymede, he would discover Rosalind's true identity. Even if Orlando already suspects that Ganymede is Rosalind, as some critics suggest he *must,* he could not very well pursue a sexual relationship with her unless they were properly married. To do so would be to compromise Rosalind's virtue and denigrate her incomparably delightful character. Besides, Rosalind's disguise is meant to be temporary yet powerful, just like the temporary yet critical move to Ardenne.

As noted previously, Elizabethans placed a great importance upon outward markers of identity such as dress and behavior. A cross-dressing woman presents a very amusing spectacle temporarily, but the ruse cannot be maintained indefinitely. Such a sustained subversion of the social order would bring chaos, and Shakespeare takes care to remind us that a woman in man's clothing is still a woman, returning to his Elizabethan audience's expectations of gendered behavior. For example, upon hearing of Orlando's trial with the lioness, Rosalind faints, prompting Oliver to remark that she lacks "a man's heart" (IV.iii.163–164), to which she responds, "So I do; but, i'faith, I should have been a woman by right" (IV.iii.173–174). This call and response signals to the audience that the game is still a game, that Ganymede is little more than a pair of pants, and that Rosalind, though smart enough to avoid temporarily her proper place in society, is ultimately willing to resume it.

The arrival of Oliver offers a second movement toward resolution. When the previously evil Oliver steps foot in Ardenne, he is transformed into the loving brother he never was before. This transformation speaks to the mutability of the human experience: people can change and, as *As You Like It* insists, can change for the better. Certainly this transformation has much to do with the movement from court into the country. Once removed from the politics and pressures of life at court, the obstacles, greed, and petty jealousies that separate the brothers dissolve. Although the play at several points satirizes the pastoral mode for its simplicity and unreality, here it indulges in the pastoral fantasy that nature can heal the wounds inflicted by the artificial and corrupt hierarchies of the man-made world.

## ACT V, SCENES I–III

### SUMMARY: ACT V, SCENE I

Touchstone and Audrey wander through the forest discussing their postponed marriage. Audrey claims that the priest was qualified to perform the ceremony, regardless of Jaques's opinion. Switching topics, Touchstone mentions that there is a youth in the forest who loves Audrey. Just then, William, the youth in question, appears. Touchstone asks William if he is witty, and William responds that he is. Touchstone then asks if William is in love with Audrey. Again, the young man responds affirmatively. When Touchstone asks William if he is educated, William admits that he is not, and Touchstone sets out to teach him a lesson. "[T]o have is to have," he says, meaning that Audrey, to whom he is engaged, is not available to other men (V.i.37). He orders William to leave, employing an exhaustive list of synonyms so that the simple lad is sure to understand him. William exits, just as Corin enters to fetch the couple on Rosalind's behalf.

### SUMMARY: ACT V, SCENE II

Orlando finds it hard to believe that Oliver has fallen so quickly and so completely in love with Aliena. Oliver vows that he has and pledges to turn over the entirety of his father's estate to Orlando once he and Aliena are married. Orlando gives his consent and orders a wedding prepared for the following day. Oliver leaves just as Rosalind, still disguised as Ganymede, arrives. Orlando confesses that though he is happy to see his brother in love, he is also pained to be without his Rosalind. Rosalind asks—with a hint of a sexual double entendre—if Ganymede cannot fill Rosalind's place, and Orlando admits that he has tired of wooing a young man in his lover's stead. Assuring Orlando that she can work magic, Rosalind promises that he will marry as he desires when Oliver takes Aliena for a bride. Just then, Phoebe and Silvius appear. Phoebe accuses Ganymede of "ungentleness," and Rosalind encourages her to devote her attentions to Silvius (V.i.67). The lovers take turns professing their various loves until Rosalind tells them to stop howling like "Irish wolves against the moon" (V.i.101–102). She promises that Ganymede will marry Phoebe on the following day if Ganymede will ever marry a woman and makes everyone promise to meet the next day at the wedding. They all agree. The group parts until Oliver's wedding.

## SUMMARY: ACT V, SCENE III

Touchstone looks forward to his marriage to Audrey on the following day. Audrey admits her excitement as well, but she hopes that her desire to be married does not compromise her chastity. The couple meets two of Duke Senior's pages. Touchstone, in a good mood, asks for a song. The pages oblige, singing of springtime and the blossoming of love. When the song ends, Touchstone claims that the song made little sense and that the music was out of tune. The pages disagree, but Touchstone is unmoved by their arguments: to him, the song was hopelessly foolish.

---

## ANALYSIS: ACT V, SCENES I–III

In the encounter between Touchstone and William, the sophistication of the court overwhelms the simplicity and ignorance of the country. But though Touchstone clearly defeats William in the country boy's attempt to win Audrey, his performance strikes us as farcical rather than triumphant. Touchstone may not be as ignorant as the uneducated country boy, but his inflated rhetoric makes him appear the more foolish of the two. Touchstone dazzles William with his city wit, for the lad lacks the means to see the ridiculousness of Touchstone's threats. But, to audiences watching Touchstone's tirade, the style and sophistication of the city may lose its luster.

In Act V, scene iii, Touchstone goes on to deflate the spiritually idealized brand of love. As the duke's pages sing a ballad that compares love to springtime, indulging every cliché from sweet lovers to trilling birds, Touchstone dismisses the song as senseless. His criticism recalls Rosalind's dismissal of literature's greatest lovers in Act IV, scene i, but it fails to convince. Whereas Rosalind's criticism seems imbued with a wide-ranging and generous understanding of the world, Touchstone's opinion seems narrow and begrudging. Although Touchstone is fundamentally correct in denying that love and budding springtime are one and the same, he remains blind to the song's undeniable beauty. Spring may not, in truth, be only a matter of "green cornfield[s]" and a "hey ding-a-ding ding," but the song captures something of the truth—the nonsense, irrationality, and sheer beauty of being in love (V.iii.16–18). One cannot expect Touchstone to see this splendor, given his rather myopic focus on the mechanics of sex. Again, his insight is most valuable as a contrast to that of Rosalind, who could well enjoy the page's song even as she absorbs its silliness.

Quick, irrational love is contagious in the Forest of Ardenne, as evidenced by Oliver's head-over-heels involvement with the disguised Celia. At court, Oliver would have no cause to notice, let alone fall in love with, a common shepherdess, but in Ardenne the injustices of class are cast aside for the sake of romance. Oliver's happy union brings about a swift end to Rosalind's game: she cannot stand to see her beloved Orlando jealous and unhappy, and so determines to hang up Ganymede's trousers. Her plan is quite clear as she strikes a marriage bargain with Phoebe, and we see the inevitability of a slew of weddings on the horizon. Some critics condemn the play at this point for what they see as a return to the normative social order that it has, thus far, delighted in subverting. As the close of the final act draws near, it is no surprise that the boys end up with the girls, and that life at court resumes, presumably, with its rigid class structures in place—in short, that all returns to normal.

## ACT V, SCENE IV & EPILOGUE

### SUMMARY: ACT V, SCENE IV
*Your 'if' is the only peacemaker; much virtue in 'if'.*
*(See* QUOTATIONS, *p. 48)*

On the following day, Duke Senior asks Orlando if he believes that Ganymede can do all that he has promised. With them, Oliver, Celia disguised as Aliena, Amiens, and Jaques have gathered to see whether the miracle of multiple marriages will be performed. Rosalind enters in her customary disguise, followed by Silvius and Phoebe. She reminds all parties of their agreements: the duke will allow Orlando to marry Rosalind, if she appears, and Phoebe will marry Ganymede unless unforeseen circumstances make her refuse, in which case she will marry Silvius. Everyone agrees, and Rosalind and Celia disappear into the forest.

While they are gone, Duke Senior notes the remarkable resemblance of Ganymede to his own daughter—an opinion that Orlando seconds. Touchstone and Audrey join the party. Touchstone entertains the company with the description of a quarrel he had. As he finishes, Rosalind and Celia return, dressed as themselves and accompanied by Hymen, the god of marriage. Phoebe, realizing that the young man she loves is, in fact, a woman, agrees to marry Silvius. Hymen marries the happy couples: Orlando and Rosalind, Oliver and Celia, Phoebe and Silvius, and Touchstone and Audrey. A great wedding feast begins.

Halfway through the festivities, Jaques de Bois, the middle brother of Oliver and Orlando, arrives with the information that Duke Frederick mounted an army to seek out Duke Senior and destroy him. As he rode toward the Forest of Ardenne, Duke Frederick met a priest who converted him to a peace-loving life. Jaques de Bois goes on to report that Frederick has abdicated his throne to his brother and has moved to a monastery. All rejoice, happy in the knowledge that they can return to the royal court. Only Jaques decides that he will not return to court. He determines to follow Duke Frederick's example and live a solitary and contemplative existence in a monastery. The wedding feast continues, and the revelers dance as everyone except Rosalind exits the stage.

## SUMMARY: EPILOGUE

*It is not the fashion to see the lady the epilogue; but it is*
*no more unhandsome than to see the lord the prologue.*
(See QUOTATIONS, p. 49)

Rosalind steps forward and admits that the play is breaking theatrical customs by allowing a female character to perform the epilogue. But the play, she says, improves with the epilogue, and so she asks the audience's indulgence. She will not beg for the audience's approval, for she is not dressed like a beggar. Instead, she will "conjure" them (Epilogue, 9). She begins with the women, asking them to like as much of the play as pleases them "for the love [they] bear to men" (Epilogue, 10–11). She asks the same of the men, saying that if she were a woman—for all the female roles in Renaissance theater were played by men—she would kiss as many of them as were handsome and hygienic. She is sure the compliment would be returned, and that the men will lavish her with applause as she curtseys.

## ANALYSIS: ACT V, SCENE IV & EPILOGUE

In the play's final act, Rosalind makes good on her promise to "make all this matter even," that is, to smooth out the remaining romantic entanglements (V.iv.18). Both Duke Senior and Orlando seem to have discovered Rosalind's game by this time, and, indeed, Orlando might well have known Ganymede's true identity from the start: "My lord, the first time that I ever saw him, / Methought he was a brother to your daughter" (V.iv.28–29). That Rosalind's identity is known before she reveals it does nothing to undermine the charm of her spell. On the contrary, her lover would not be any less willing than the audience to play along with her charms.

Rosalind's love for Orlando requires the blessing of marriage in order to have currency in the world beyond the forest. Hymen, by his own declaration, is a god not of the forest but "of every town," and it is to town that the lovers will now return (V.iv.135). This movement should not be read as a simple victory of city over country, especially when we consider that one location necessitates the other: only a respite in the country could mend what civilization had broken. Although *As You Like It* draws discernable lines between the merits of town and country, heterosexual and homosexual unions, artifice and nature, youth and age, and idealism and realism, it refuses to take a definitive stand on any issue. Rather, the play insists on the complexity of life by allowing for the crossing of such boundaries. The characters' delight in transcending these boundaries suggests a utopia where human existence is no less joyous for all its absurdities and hardships, and one where all that has been broken can, to some degree, be rebuilt. The play's hopeful vision is one in which not everyone can or will share, as the implacable Jaques makes clear, but it is one to which most of us are only too delighted to cling.

The Epilogue, in which one of the actors remains onstage after the play has ended, was a standard part of many plays in Elizabethan times. An epilogue proves a convenient way to tie up loose ends, to distill the thematic concerns of the play into a neat speech, and to ask the audience for applause. But Shakespeare explodes the conventions of the form when he allows Rosalind to take the stage. Not only has Rosalind dropped her disguise as Ganymede, but the boy actor playing Rosalind lets slip the mask of Rosalind. When he solicits the approval of the men in the audience, he says, "If I were a woman I would kiss as many of you as had beards that pleased me" (Epilogue, 14–16). The dizzying intermingling of homosexual and heterosexual affections that govern a man pretending to be woman pretending to be a man pretending to be a woman in the hopes of seducing a man reiterates the play's celebration of the wonderful complexities of human life.

# Important Quotations Explained

1.  Now, my co-mates and brothers in exile,
    Hath not old custom made this life more sweet
    Than that of painted pomp? Are not these woods
    More free from peril than the envious court?
    Here feel we not the penalty of Adam,
    The seasons' difference, as the icy fang
    And churlish chiding of the winter's wind,
    Which when it bites and blows upon my body
    Even till I shrink with cold, I smile, and say
    'This is no flattery. These are counsellors
    That feelingly persuade me what I am.'
    Sweet are the uses of adversity
    Which, like the toad, ugly and venomous,
    Wears yet a precious jewel in his head;
    And this our life, exempt from public haunt,
    Finds tongues in trees, books in the running brooks,
    Sermons in stones, and good in everything.
    (II.i.1–17)

These lines, spoken by Duke Senior upon his introduction in Act II, scene i, establish the pastoral mode of the play. With great economy, Shakespeare draws a dividing line between the "painted pomp" of court—with perils great enough to drive the duke and his followers into exile—and the safe and restorative Forest of Ardenne (II.i.3). The woods are romanticized, as they typically are in pastoral literature, and the mood is set for the remainder of the play. Although perils may present themselves, they remain distant, and, in the end, there truly is "good in everything" (II.i.17). This passage, more than any other in the play, presents the conceits of the pastoral mode. Here, the corruptions of life at court are left behind in order to learn the simple and valuable lessons of the country. Shakespeare highlights the educational, edifying, and enlightening nature of this foray into the woods by employing language that invokes the classroom, the library, and the church: in the trees, brooks, and stones surrounding him, the duke finds tongues, books, and sermons. As is his wont, Shakespeare goes on to complicate the literary conventions upon which he depends. His shepherds and shepherdesses, for instance, ultimately prove too lovesick or dim-witted to dole out the kind of wisdom the pastoral form demands of them, but for now Shakespeare merely sets up the opposition between city and country that provides the necessary tension to drive his story forward.

2.　　As I do live by food, I met a fool,
　　　　Who laid him down and basked him in the sun,
　　　　And railed on Lady Fortune in good terms,
　　　　In good set terms, and yet a motley fool.
　　　　'Good morrow, fool,' quoth I. 'No, sir,' quoth he,
　　　　'Call me not fool till heaven hath sent me fortune.'
　　　　And then he drew a dial from his poke,
　　　　And looking on it with lack-lustre eye
　　　　Says very wisely 'It is ten o'clock.'
　　　　'Thus we may see', quoth he, 'how the world wags.
　　　　'Tis but an hour ago since it was nine,
　　　　And after one hour more 'twill be eleven.
　　　　And so from hour to hour we ripe and ripe,
　　　　And then from hour to hour we rot and rot;
　　　　And thereby hangs a tale.'
　　　　　　　　(II.vii.14–28)

In Act II, scene vii, melancholy Jaques displays an uncharacteristic burst of delight. While wandering through the forest, he relates, he met a fool, who entertained him with rather nihilistic musings on the passage of time and man's life. According to Touchstone, time ensures nothing other than man's own decay: "from hour to hour we rot and rot" (II.vii.27). That this speech appeals to Jaques says much about his character: he delights not only in the depressing, but also in the rancid. Practically all of Touchstone's lines contain some bawdy innuendo, and these are no exception. Here, by punning the word "hour" with "whore," he transforms the general notion of man's decay into the unpleasant specifics of a man dying from venereal disease. Touchstone appropriately, if distastefully, confirms this hidden meaning by ending his speech with the words "thereby hangs a tale," for tale was Elizabethan slang for penis (II.vii.28).

3.　　No, faith; die by attorney. The poor world is almost six
　　　　thousand years old, and in all this time there was not any

man died in his own person, videlicet, in a love-cause.
Troilus had his brains dashed out with a Grecian club, yet he
did what he could to die before, and he is one of the patterns
of love. Leander, he would have lived many a fair year
though Hero had turned nun if it had not been for a hot
midsummer night, for, good youth, he went but forth to
wash him in the Hellespont and, being taken with the
cramp, was drowned; and the foolish chroniclers of that age
found it was Hero of Sestos. But these are all lies. Men have
died from time to time, and worms have eaten them, but not
for love.

> (IV.i.81–92)

In Act IV, scene i, Rosalind rejects Orlando's claim that he would die
if Rosalind should fail to return his love. Rosalind's insistence that
"[m]en have died from time to time, and worms have eaten them,
but not for love" is one of the most recognizable lines from the play
and perhaps the wisest (IV.i.91–92). Here, Rosalind takes on one of
the most dominant interpretations of romantic love, an understanding that is sustained by mythology and praised in literature, and
insists on its unreality. She holds to the light the stories of Troilus
and Leander, both immortal lovers, in order to expose their falsity.
Men are, according to Rosalind, much more likely to die by being
hit with a club or drowning than in a fatal case of heartbreak. Rosalind does not mean to deny the existence of love. On the contrary, she
delights in loving Orlando. Instead, her criticism comes from an
unwillingness to let affection cloud or warp her sense of reality. By
casting aside the conventions of the standard—and usually tragic—
romance, Rosalind advocates a kind of love that belongs and can
survive in the real world that she inhabits.

4.  O sir, we quarrel in print, by the book, as you have books for
    good manners. I will name you the degrees. The first, the
    Retort Courteous; the second, the Quip Modest; the third,
    the Reply Churlish; the fourth, the Reproof Valiant; the
    fifth, the Countercheck Quarrelsome; the sixth, the Lie with
    Circumstance; the seventh, the Lie Direct. All these you may
    avoid but the Lie Direct; and you may avoid that, too, with
    an 'if'. I knew when seven justices could not take up a
    quarrel, but when the parties were met themselves, one of
    them thought but of an 'if', as 'If you said so, then I said so',

and they shook hands and swore brothers. Your 'if' is the only peacemaker; much virtue in 'if'.
(V.iv.81–92)

In Act V, scene iv, Touchstone delivers an account of a recent argument he has had. His anatomy of the quarrel, as this speech might be called, is a deftly comic moment that skewers all behavior that is "by the book," whether it be rules for engaging an enemy or a lover (V.iv.81). The end of the speech, in which Touchstone turns his attentions to the powers of the word "if," is particularly fine and fitting. "If" points to the potential of events in possible worlds. "If" allows slights to be forgiven, wounds to be salved, and promising opportunities to be taken. Notably, within a dozen lines of this speech, Duke Senior, Orlando, and Phoebe each usher in a new stage of life with a simple sentence that begins with that simple word.

5.    It is not the fashion to see the lady the epilogue; but it is no more unhandsome than to see the lord the prologue. If it be true that good wine needs no bush, 'tis true that a good play needs no epilogue. Yet to good wine they do use good bushes, and good plays prove the better by the help of good epilogues. What a case am I in then, that am neither a good epilogue nor cannot insinuate with you in the behalf of a good play! I am not furnished like a beggar, therefore to beg will not become me. My way is to conjure you; and I'll begin with the women. I charge you, O women, for the love you bear to men, to like as much of this play as please you. And I charge you, O men, for the love you bear to women—as I perceive by your simpering none of you hates them— that between you and the women the play may please. If I were a woman I would kiss as many of you as had beards that pleased me, complexions that liked me, and breaths that I defied not. And I am sure, as many as have good beards, or good faces, or sweet breaths will for my kind offer, when I make curtsy, bid me farewell.
(Epilogue, 1–19).

The Epilogue was a standard component of Elizabethan drama. One actor remains onstage after the play has ended to ask the audience for applause. As Rosalind herself notes, it is odd that she has been chosen to deliver the Epilogue, as that task is usually assigned

QUOTATIONS

to a male character. By the time she addresses the audience directly, Rosalind has discarded her Ganymede disguise. She is again a woman and has married a man. Although we may think the play of gender has come to an end with the fall of the curtain, we must remember that women were forbidden to perform onstage in Shakespeare's England. Rosalind would have been played by a man, which further obscures the boundaries of gender. Rosalind emerges as a man who pretends to be a woman who pretends to be a man who pretends to be a woman to win the love of a man. When the actor solicits the approval of the men in the audience, he says, "If I were a woman I would kiss as many of you as had beards that pleased me"— returning us to the dizzying intermingling of homosexual and heterosexual affections that govern life in the Forest of Ardenne (Epilogue, 14–16). The theater, like Ardenne, is an escape from reality where the wonderful, sometimes overwhelmingcomplexities of human life can be witnessed, contemplated, enjoyed, and studied.

QUOTATIONS

# KEY FACTS

FULL TITLE
*As You Like It*

AUTHOR
William Shakespeare

TYPE OF WORK
Play

GENRE
Comedy, pastoral

LANGUAGE
English

TIME AND PLACE WRITTEN
1598–1600; London, England

DATE OF FIRST PUBLICATION
First published in the Folio of 1623

PUBLISHER
Isaac Jaggard and Edmund Blount

TONE
Comic, romantic

SETTING (TIME)
Sixteenth century

SETTING (PLACE)
France, primarily the fictional Forest of Ardenne

PROTAGONIST
Rosalind

MAJOR CONFLICT
Rosalind and Orlando fall in love, but Rosalind is unjustly banished from Duke Frederick's court; Orlando is both denied his birthright by his jealous brother Oliver and forced to flee from the vindictive Duke Frederick.

RISING ACTION
In order to teach Orlando how to be a proper husband to her, Rosalind disguises herself as a young man named Ganymede and instructs him in the ways of love.

CLIMAX
Rosalind promises to marry Orlando and gets Phoebe to agree to marry Silvius, should things go awry with her beloved Ganymede, who is actually Rosalind in disguise.

FALLING ACTION
Rosalind, appearing as herself, marries Orlando, and Phoebe marries Silvius.

THEMES
The delights of love; the malleability of the human experience; city life versus country life

MOTIFS
Artifice; homoeroticism; exile

SYMBOLS
Orlando's poems; the slain deer; Ganymede

FORESHADOWING
Rosalind's uncharacteristically awkward first encounter with Orlando anticipates the depth of her affection for him.

KEY FACTS

# STUDY QUESTIONS &
ESSAY TOPICS

## STUDY QUESTIONS

1.  *By putting on male clothes and adopting a masculine
    swagger, Rosalind easily passes as a man throughout the
    better part of the play. What does her behavior suggest
    about gender? Does the play imply that notions of
    gender are fixed or fluid? Explain.*

Rosalind's behavior suggests that she knows better than anyone else
that her society makes different demands of men and women. For
instance, she knows that, when dressed as Ganymede, she is forbidden from crying over a perceived slight from Orlando. Likewise,
something as simple as a "doublet and hose"—her male disguise—
stops her from celebrating the discovery that Orlando has authored
love poems in her honor (III.ii.200–201). Indeed, as the clothes
make the man, they also make the woman act like one. To Elizabethans, the fundamental divide between the sexes may have been as
much a matter of external expressions of behavior and clothing as of
anatomy. On one hand, this conception made gender a much more
fluid notion than it is to many modern audiences. Codes of behavior
were more a matter of mimicry than a function of chromosomal
makeup, which Rosalind shows as she plays a swaggering young
man imitating a woman.

   On the other hand, this fluidity caused a great deal of anxiety
among Elizabethans, who, in the end, wanted very much to believe
that the categories that organized their world were stable. Thus,
they insisted that certain behaviors and customs were established by
one's sex. Women might pretend to be men for a brief and entertaining moment, but they must, in the end, behave like women. Rosalind eases the anxieties surrounding her very deft performance by
reverting, time and again, to the behaviors expected of her as a
woman: to the Elizabethan mind, she would be a much more troubling character if she did not faint at the sight of Orlando's blood.
Although gender proves to be completely undefined in the Forest of

Ardenne, everyone is returned to his or her supposedly proper place by the final act. Indeed, nowhere is the anxiety over gender-swapping quelled more than in the Epilogue, where the actor playing Rosalind, who is herself so talented at role-playing, unveils himself as an actor, thereby promising that with his bow comes an end to subversion and a return to the established social order.

2. *Discuss* As You Like It *as an example of pastoral literature. What features of the pastoral mode lend themselves to social criticism? What, if anything, does Shakespeare's play criticize?*

Pastoral literature primarily establishes a contrast between life in the city and life in the country, and suggests that the intense concerns of court life can be rectified by a brief foray into nature. The neat and convenient division between town and country allows characters the distance required to contemplate, criticize, and reform city life. *As You Like It* certainly acknowledges this convention: urban life, as governed by the likes of Duke Frederick and Oliver, is plagued with injustices, and the Forest of Ardenne allows Duke Senior, Rosalind, Orlando, and the rest not only to escape oppression but to build the foundation of a more loving and just society. But Shakespeare does not content himself with criticizing the court and romanticizing the country. Instead, he trains a careful—and comic—eye on the entire pastoral tradition. Although Shakespeare's urban sophisticates find solace in Ardenne and manage to heal the wounds inflicted on them by vengeful dukes and unfair customs, the green world they encounter is not a paradise, peopled as it is with the likes of Silvius and Audrey. The former is blinded by love, the latter by her own dim wits, and neither is insightful enough to lead the exiles toward a completely redeemed life.

3. *Throughout the play, we find numerous allusions to cuckoldry. In a play that celebrates love and ends with four marriages, what purpose might these allusions serve?*

In Act IV, scene ii, Jaques and Duke Senior's loyal followers decorate a hunter with his slain deer and sing a song meant to calm any anxieties men might feel regarding unfaithful wives. All men, the song says, have suffered the indignity of wearing the cuckold's horns—the symbol of having an adulterous wife—and so it is no indignity: "Take thou no scorn to wear the horn" (IV.ii.14). Frequent mentions of cuckoldry were not uncommon on the Elizabethan stage. There are several reasons for these references. Of course, they spoke to an anxiety not uncommon in any patriarchal society—namely, that women's sexual appetites could not be controlled, thereby potentially undermining the entire social order. In *As You Like It*, the frequent mention of cuckoldry contributes to the play's investment in disabusing its characters and its audience of the untenable nature of the perfect romance. Although Touchstone's words are considerably cruder than Rosalind's, the clown's insistence that "[a]s horns are odious, they are necessary" serves much the same purpose as his mistress's reminder to Orlando that women change for the worse once they are married: it reminds the lovers that real love, because it is obtainable and human, is far from perfect (III.iii.42).

## SUGGESTED ESSAY TOPICS

1. *As You Like It is full of characters pretending to be someone other than themselves. To what degree are the characters aware that they are role-playing? Does their acting have serious consequences, or is it merely a game?*

2. *Like Rosalind, both Touchstone and Jaques possess an ability to see things that the other characters do not. They are critics, but their criticism differs greatly from Rosalind's. How is this so? To what effect do these different criticisms lead?*

3. *In a play that ends with the formation and celebration of a community, we may be struck by Jaques's decision not to return to court. What does his refusal suggest about his character? What effect does it have on the play's ending? Does it cast a shadow over an otherwise happy ending, or is it inconsequential?*

4. *As You Like It explores the possibility of both homosexual and heterosexual attraction. Does the play present one as the antithesis of the other, or does it suggest a more complex*

relationship between the two? What, in the end, does the play have to say about these different forms of love?

5.   What does Phoebe represent? Why does Rosalind react so negatively toward her?

6.   What is the significance of Duke Frederick's unexpected and very sudden change in Act V? Discuss this episode in relation to other transformations in the play. What does As You Like It suggest about the malleability of the human experience?

# REVIEW & RESOURCES

## QUIZ

1.  According to Oliver, what would Orlando bring to a wrestling match with Charles?

    A.  A strong competitive edge
    B.  A lust for prize money
    C.  Poison, or some other deceitful means of securing victory
    D.  An comprehensive knowledge of strategicphysical combat

2.  Why does Oliver inherit the bulk of his father's estate?

    A.  Oliver was the son least able to make his own way in the world.
    B.  Oliver is the oldest son, and therefore guaranteed the inheritance by law.
    C.  Oliver is the more loving than his brothers.
    D.  Oliver doctors his father's will.

3.  At what event do Orlando and Rosalind meet?

    A.  The wedding of Duke Frederick
    B.  A wrestling match
    C.  A public execution
    D.  A traveling circus

4.  What name does Rosalind assume for her disguised self?

    A.  Ganymede
    B.  Jove
    C.  Harry
    D.  Icarus

5.   Why does Duke Frederick dislike Orlando?

    A.   Orlando finds Rosalind more beautiful than the duke's own daughter, Celia.

    B.   Orlando's brother, Oliver, owes the duke aconsiderable sum of money.

    C.   Orlando beat the duke's prized wrestler, Charles.

    D.   The duke and Orlando's father were enemies.

6.   Upon his introduction in Act II, scene i, Duke Senior gathers his loyal followers in the Forest of Ardenne for what purpose?

    A.   To hunt deer

    B.   To mount an army against Duke Frederick

    C.   To swim in the brook

    D.   To tease the melancholy Jaques

7.   How does Duke Frederick plan to find Celia and Rosalind after their departure from court?

    A.   He will interview every person in his castle until someone confesses information as to hisdaughter's whereabouts

    B.   He will recruit Oliver to help find Orlando, whom he suspects has teamed up with the women

    C.   He will assume a disguise and go looking for them himself in the Forest of Ardenne

    D.   He has no plans to find them, and is glad theyare gone

8.   On what topic does Corin attempt to council the young shepherd, Silvius?

    A.   The maintenance of the flock

    B.   The politics of court life

    C.   Love

    D.   Friendship

9. Upon arriving in the Forest of Ardenne, Adam claims that he will soon die. What does he assume the cause of his death will be?

    A. Old age
    B. Hunger
    C. Lovesickness
    D. Gout

10. After an eye-opening stroll around the Forest of Ardenne, what profession does Jaques intend to pursue?

    A. A shepherd
    B. A highwayman
    C. A fool
    D. A butler

11. How much time does Duke Frederick allow Oliver to find Orlando?

    A. One year
    B. One month
    C. One week
    D. A fortnight

12. What does the disguised Rosalind promise to do for Orlando?

    A. Woo Rosalind on his behalf
    B. Help him to overthrow his brother, Oliver
    C. Help him to overcome his lovesickness
    D. Provide him and Adam with shelter

13. Why does Rosalind doubt that Orlando is truly in love?

    A. Love is a madness, and he does not look like a madman.
    B. His poems are poorly rhymed and measured.
    C. She has heard him claim to be in love with countless girls.
    D. He is too young to know what love is.

14. What does Silvius say of Phoebe's eyes?

    A.   They are so amorous that they embarrass him.
    B.   They are so dull that they bore him.
    C.   They are so beautiful that they intimidate him.
    D.   They are so scornful that they will murder him.

15. Why does Rosalind believe that Phoebe should feel lucky?

    A.   Her father has willed her a fortune, allowing her to marry whomever she chooses.
    B.   A man like Silvius loves her, despite her lack of beauty.
    C.   She has no lover and therefore her heart will neverbe broken.
    D.   By living in the forest, she is spared the cruel politicsof life at court.

16. How does Phoebe respond to Ganymede's harsh criticism of her?

    A.   She poisons his wine.
    B.   She disguises herself as royalty in hopes of putting him in his place.
    C.   She writes him a love letter.
    D.   She employs Charles the wrestler to beat him up.

17. Whom does Orlando save from the attack of a hungry lioness?

    A.   His brother, Oliver
    B.   Duke Senior
    C.   Silvius, the shepherd
    D.   His long-lost father, Sir Rowland de Bois

18. What does Rosalind do after learning of Orlando's injury?

    A.   She faints.
    B.   She pens him an angry but concerned letter, tellinghim to be more careful.
    C.   She weeps at the thought of losing him.
    D.   She delivers a cutting speech about the ridiculousnessof bravery.

19. How does Rosalind respond to Orlando when he contends that he will die unless she returns his love?

    A. She favorably compares him to the great lovers of classical literature.
    B. She vows to kill herself before his dying body hitsthe ground.
    C. She suggests that she is not worthy of such devotion.
    D. She assures him that no man has ever died for love.

20. What animal do Jaques and the lords of the forest kill?

    A. A deer
    B. An antelope
    C. A bear
    D. A squirrel

21. Which inhabitant of the forest and admirer of Audrey does Touchstone rudely dismiss?

    A. Jaques
    B. William
    C. Oliver Martext
    D. Corin

22. With whom does Oliver fall in love?

    A. Rosalind
    B. Phoebe
    C. Aliena
    D. Audrey

23. To what does Rosalind compare the declarations of love from Orlando, Silvius, and Phoebe?

    A. The music of the spheres
    B. The howling of Irish wolves
    C. The greatest poetry of Ovid
    D. The sound of mourners following a hearse

24. Why does Duke Frederick abandon his plan to mount an army and attack Duke Senior?

    A.   His followers abandon him, and he lacks the strength to wage a successful campaign.

    B.   He finds a carving of his brother's image and is overcome by sentimental memories of their childhood together.

    C.   He marries a beautiful woman who convinces him not to be such an angry person.

    D.   He meets a religious man on his way to the forest who converts him to a peaceful life.

25. Who decides not to return to court?

    A.   Jaques

    B.   Celia

    C.   Duke Frederick

    D.   Oliver

# Suggestions for Further Reading

BAMBER, LINDA. *Comic Women, Tragic Men: A Study of Gender and Genre in Shakespeare*. Stanford: Stanford University Press, 1982.

BERRY, RALPH. *Shakespeare's Comic Rites*. Cambridge: Cambridge University Press, 1984.

BLOOM, HAROLD, ed. *Modern Critical Interpretations: William Shakespeare's As You Like It*. New York: Chelsea House Publishers, 1988.

CARROLL, WILLIAM C. *The Metamorphoses of Shakespearean Comedy*. Princeton: Princeton University Press, 1985.

FRYE, NORTHROP. *A Natural Perspective: The Development of Shakespearean Comedy and Romance*. New York: Columbia University Press, 1965.

HALIO, JAY L. *Twentieth Century Interpretations of As You Like It: A Collection of Critical Essays*. Englewood Cliffs, New Jersey: Prentice-Hall, Inc., 1968.

LEGGATT, ALEXANDER. *Shakespeare's Comedy of Love*. London: Methuen, 1974.

WHEELER, RICHARD. *Shakespeare's Development and the Problem Comedies: Turn and Counter-Turn*. Berkeley and Los Angeles: University of California Press, 1981.

YOUNG, DAVID. *The Heart's Forest: A Study of Shakespeare's Pastoral Plays*. New Haven: Yale University Press, 1976.

REVIEW & RESOURCES

# SparkNotes
# Test Preparation
# Guides

The SparkNotes team figured it was time to cut standardized tests
down to size. We've studied the tests for you, so that SparkNotes
test prep guides are:

## Smarter
Packed with critical-thinking skills and test-
taking strategies that will improve your score.

## Better
Fully up to date, covering all new features of the tests,
with study tips on every type of question.

## Faster
Our books cover exactly what you need to
know for the test. No more, no less.

# SPARKNOTES™ LITERATURE GUIDES